# I Know My Child
# Can Do Better!

# I Know My Child Can Do Better!

*A Frustrated Parent's Guide to Educational Options*

ANNE RAMBO, PH.D.

with Teacher Tips by Julie Little, M.S.

**Contemporary Books**

Chicago  New York  San Francisco  Lisbon  London  Madrid  Mexico City
Milan  New Delhi  San Juan  Seoul  Singapore  Sydney  Toronto

**Library of Congress Cataloging-in-Publication Data**

Rambo, Anne Hearon.
   I know my child can do better: a frustrated parent's guide to educational
options / Anne Hearon Rambo.
        p.   cm.
   Includes bibliographical references.
   ISBN 0-8092-9452-4
   1. School choice—United States—Handbooks, manuals, etc.
 I. Title.
   LB1027.9.R34   2001
   379.1'11'0973—dc21                      2001028187

## Contemporary Books

*A Division of The **McGraw-Hill** Companies*

1 2 3 4 5 6 7 8 9 0   AGM/AGM   0 9 8 7 6 5 4 3 2 1

ISBN 0-8092-9452-4

This book was set in Sabon
Printed and bound by Quebecor Martinsburg

Cover and interior design by Nick Panos
Cover photograph copyright © Larry Dale Gordon/The Image Bank
Interior illustrations copyright © EyeWire, Inc.

McGraw-Hill books are available at special quantity discounts to use as premiums
and sales promotions, or for use in corporate training programs. For more
information, please write to the Director of Special Sales, Professional Publishing,
McGraw-Hill, Two Penn Plaza, New York, NY 10121-2298. Or contact your local
bookstore.

This book is printed on acid-free paper.

# Contents

# Foreword

As an elementary school principal for twenty years, I saw firsthand the conflicts that can arise when parents and school administrators disagree on what is best for a child. Add to this the inevitable conflicts children have with one another and may have with particular teachers, and the situation indeed becomes complex. In 1993, I founded the first school system–based office for conflict resolution in the United States. Ultimately, I contributed to the development of more than 100 school mediation programs, and in 1994 I received the first annual Society of Professionals in Dispute Resolution award for advancing the cause of dispute resolution in education.

My background led me to take a keen interest in Dr. Rambo's book. I know that many parents are ill-equipped to advocate for their children and either suffer in silence as their children receive a less than optimal education or engage in pointless battles with school officials. There is nothing those of us who are education professionals would rather see than informed, active, committed parents, who can help us help their children; we all win when parents can do their job well.

This book should be recquired reading for every parent with a school-age child. While the book is easy to read, irreverent, and even funny, the information presented is quite serious and could make a huge difference in your child's life. Without this kind of clear, practical advice, your child will have to struggle along in school without you, for better or worse. With this book in hand, you will be well-equipped to be your child's supporter, counselor, and advocate, throughout his or her educational career. Make a difference; read this book and get involved.

Marcia Sweedler, Ph.D.
Director, Coalition for Conflict Resolution in Education

# Acknowledgments

I was inspired to write this book by the many concerned parents I have seen in family therapy, all of whom want the best for their children. Along the way, the book was greatly helped by my agent, Ann Rittenberg, who believed in the project even when I did not; my editors at Contemporary Books; my colleagues at Nova Southeastern University, at Henderson Mental Health Center, and in the Broward County School District; my parents, Shelby Hearon and Bill Halpern and Bob and Genevieve Hearon; and my brother, Reed Hearon, along with the many schoolteachers in my family—especially my stepmother, Genevieve Tarlton Hearon; my aunts Marcia Hearon Lind, Susan Reed Smith, and Linda Reed Sanford; and my cousin Julie Little, whose comments you will read in this book. The book and I both enjoyed the loving encouragement of my best friend and husband, Irving Rosenbaum, and the real-life adventures thoughtfully provided by our children, Danielle, Matthew, Alison, and Marissa Rosenbaum and Rachel Rambo.

Julie wishes to acknowledge the many excellent teachers she has worked with in her years in education. Together, Julie and I thank our interview subjects. And together we dedicate the book to our mutual grandmother, Evelyn Roberts Reed, in whose home books and children were always welcome.

# Introduction

## *You Are Not Alone!*

Has your child, like Max, ever been unhappy and restless in school? Max's kindergarten teacher tells his mother that although Max is on track academically, his behavior is often disruptive. Typically, the teacher reports, Max finishes his own work quickly. Then, while the other children are still working, he starts to fidget in his seat. Eventually he progresses to talking to the other children, interrupting their work. Sometimes he even does somersaults in the aisles. The teacher says that Max lacks discipline, and hints at possible problems caused by his not having a father in the home. Feeling worried and guilty, Max's mother recently signed him up for karate lessons, hoping the activity's structure would be useful to him. But the only result was that Max now karate-kicks the other children's desks when he gets bored.

Has your child, like Sally, ever been teased? Sally doesn't want to go to eighth grade because the other children tease her. When Sally's parents consulted the school's guidance counselor, they were told that all children get teased from time to time and that

they should not give in to Sally's excuses. The counselor did tell them to let her know if the situation worsened, but Sally's parents aren't sure how to recognize when Sally's distress escalates. They have assumed Sally must be doing better, since she has stopped complaining and talking about what is happening at school. Actually, a jealous classmate has started a rumor that Sally is gay. With the homophobia that is characteristic, unfortunately, of this young teenage group, her peers have responded by ostracizing her entirely. Sally doesn't know what to do or say to combat the whispers she hears constantly around her.

Or do you have a child like Justin, who just doesn't see the point in school? Justin is sixteen and wants to drop out of school. School has always been a struggle for him; he feels he has to work harder than his peers to accomplish the same tasks. Although Justin is the guy everyone in the neighborhood turns to for advice on cars or how to fix a broken appliance, the kind of work he is given in school doesn't fit him as well. He has difficulties with reading and writing, although no specific learning disability has been diagnosed. Nonetheless, with strong parental backing and hard work, he has managed to maintain a C average. With college not a goal for him at this point, though, he is questioning the utility of keeping up this hard work through high school. Justin's father gives him an impassioned speech about the importance of a high school degree, asking as well if he wants to spend the rest of his life working at fast-food restaurants. However, when Justin asks around about what kind of job he could get with a high school degree, he finds he would be working in—fast food restaurants.

These situations are drawn from my work with school-age children and their families. The problems are different, but their solution was the same: all of these parents needed to know more about how the system really works. Max's mother didn't know that Max was intellectually gifted and needed a special enrichment program to keep him from being bored. She thought the teacher would know if there was anything special about Max's abilities, but in fact, teachers at the kindergarten level are able to identify the gifted children in their classrooms with only 4.3 percent accuracy.[1] Max was identified as a gifted child only *after* he had been held back in kindergarten, a mistake that cost him a year and made him even more bored in first grade.

Sally's parents went for help only *after* Sally had made a serious, but fortunately aborted, suicide attempt. Nationwide, approximately 30 percent of all teen suicides are attributed to social pressure regarding sexual identity.[2] Typically, school officials are unaware of harassment or teasing about this issue.

Justin and his father didn't know that Justin could attend a private vocational school and get his high school degree together with the certification in air-conditioning repair he wants. He could pay for this schooling with federally insured student loans at a low interest rate. Should he wish to pursue further education, he could enter a community college and then transfer to a four-year college. Furthermore, if he is not interested in additional education (or not interested in pursuing it right away), at least he would have a viable credential for getting what he would consider a "real" job.

Children who dislike and avoid school—and their concerned parents—make up most of my clientele. The first thing I say to parents who come to me for help is something worth repeating now: *Yes, the system really is more complicated now than when you were in school.* Let's take a look at why that is and at how important it is that you keep exerting the effort to make school right for your child.

Remember Muncie, Indiana? Back in 1927, it was dubbed "Middletown" in Robert and Helen Lynd's classic sociological study of industrial America.[3] For decades it stood as a symbol of the heartland, a thriving blue-collar community. But Muncie is dying today. Its five factories have all shut down, and the service jobs (at fast-food restaurants, motels, and the local hospital) that its former factory workers now hold pay only about a quarter as much as the earlier work. Thousands have left town to look for jobs elsewhere. Yet, ironically, the new software company in town can't find enough people to hire. It needs workers with more education.

Muncie is not an isolated example. The U.S. Bureau of Labor estimates that 80 percent of the jobs created in the next decade will require familiarity with technology we don't have today, technology even now being invented.[4] Constant change in our workplaces rewards those who in adult life keep the zest for learning that nearly all children have when they start school. Too many negative school experiences take away that enthusiasm. Despite the complexity of the task, it has never been more important for parents to become involved in their children's education. This book will show you how to do so wisely.

## Why Are Things So Complicated?

Before getting too far, let's ask the important question of what makes schooling so much more complicated these days.

### Families Are Changing Faster than Schools Can Adapt

During the past forty years, the percentage of women in the workforce has grown from around 25 to 58.3 percent; this growth has been most striking for younger women with children at home, over 60 percent of whom are now in the workforce. The days when Mom had time to drop by school and volunteer in the classroom are largely past. During the same time period, the rate of divorce has grown from one of every six marriages to one of every two marriages. Forty percent of all school-age children in the United States now live apart from their biological fathers.[5] Most teachers and school administrators, however, like most of the rest of us, grew up with a more traditional model of family life. Working parents, single parents, remarried parents, and those with a less traditional family structure may find themselves excluded (like Fred) or unfairly blamed for their child's difficulties (like Doreen). Children from intact two-parent families (like Jim and Patsy's) may be assumed to be doing fine, even when they are not.

## Teachers Don't Have So Much Authority

Forty years ago, rightly or wrongly, teachers were much freer to utilize whatever disciplinary techniques worked for them. Children could be suspended or expelled with greater ease than they are today, and the parents of children with special needs were routinely told that the neighborhood public school could not educate their children. Legal changes have produced a much greater awareness of potential liability on the part of both teachers and school administrators. Teachers today can be and have been sued for such a time-honored practice as rapping a child on the knuckles with a ruler. School principals, having learned to brace for legal consequences, monitor teachers more closely. They are also far more reluctant to suspend or expel a child. Turning a child away from public education altogether is now against the law. Private schools retain a greater freedom to refuse children admission and to expel them, but they, too, operate within circumscribed limits, and the constraints on teacher behavior apply to private-school settings as well. All these factors mean that teachers and school officials assign a greater share of responsibility to parents than in the past, if only by default. To cite just one concrete example, district officials in the school district in which I live and work recently instructed teachers to promote children from elementary to middle school by a certain age, whether or not they show academic readiness. This policy is in response to discipline problems and a fear of lawsuits. When I asked what would happen to a child who was promoted to middle school and could not keep up, I was told, "Well, the parent would need to complain, and then we could make an exception." Parents who do not know to complain, or who hold back so they don't appear "pushy," may indeed find (like Jim and Patsy) that their children get lost in the crowd.

## There's So Much More to Learn—and to Teach

My third-grade teacher, back in 1964, taught a class of twenty-five children, all of whom lived close to the school, most of them within walking distance. The children were in school from 8 A.M. until 2 P.M. If a child became disruptive, that youngster could be sent to the principal's office to stay until the mother came to take him home. Every child in the class could function more or less at a third-grade level, and no special accommodations were made. The teacher's primary focus for the year was teaching the multiplication tables. In my child's third-grade class, in 1998, there were also twenty-five children. But there the similarities end. Very few of her classmates lived near the school, and parents could not be called to pick up children during the school day—most parents work during that time. Teachers were expected to handle their own classroom behavior problems. Of the twenty-five children in my daughter's class, about a third went to some form of special education during the school day—to an enrichment class for the gifted, speech and language training, remedial reading, or a special class for the learning disabled. In addition, her teacher had to wear a microphone and accommodate her curriculum to accommodate the hearing- and vision-impaired children mainstreamed in her classroom.

The school day itself now stretches from 7 A.M., when the first children arrive to get breakfast at school, until 6 P.M., when the last children are picked up from the on-site after-care program run by the school. In addition to the multiplication tables, the third-grade curriculum now includes such delicate subjects as peaceful conflict resolution, cultural-diversity sensitivity training, the benefits of the free enterprise system, saying no to drugs, and how to avoid contracting the HIV virus (all mandated subjects for the third grade in Florida—many states with a more liberal state legislature require still additional "public service" topics). With so many objectives to meet, it is not reasonable to expect a teacher to make your individual child's needs her first priority. That responsibility falls back to the parent.

## The Stakes Are Higher than Ever

Forty years ago, someone with a high school degree and no particular skills could get a job that paid reasonably well and held the possibility for future promotion, say, in helping to manufacture cars or make steel. Today those jobs are automated. Jobs for printers and telephone operators, two other fields that used to require a general high school degree and would provide a reasonable living, are diminishing as desktop publishing and computerized communication replace them. U.S. Bureau of Labor statistics indicate that present and future growth areas are in computer programming, database analysis, the allied health professions, and engineering. Some 1.3 million more jobs than applicants are predicted over the next decade in the area of general information technology.[6] These are all jobs requiring considerable education and training as well as the ability to continue lifelong learning, to keep up with rapid changes in technology. Increasingly, those unable or unwilling to keep up with the demands of the information age are relegated to low-paying service jobs in fast-food restaurants and malls.

## What's a Parent to Do?

The good news is you have more options today than parents did in the past—as well as more responsibility. Today parents have *greater possibilities* to take charge of their children's education.

### New Federal Laws

The Education for All Handicapped Children Act (PL 94-142), first passed in 1975 and subsequently renamed (and reaffirmed as) the Individuals with Disabilities Education Act (IDEA; PL 105-17), requires that public school districts turn away no child and provide for every child the type of education he or she needs.[7] This means, for example, that Fred can request and receive testing for his child, even when the teacher does not think it's indicated. Psychological testing is one of the services that schools are now legally bound to provide. If Fred's child is found to have a special need, she would fall under the full provisions of the act. The school is legally bound to provide whatever service she might need, from remedial instruction to overcome a learning disability to a special lunch time because of her low blood sugar. Most parents have no idea how broad ranging are their rights. But public school teachers and administrators are well aware of these legal provisions, and will yield to appropriate pressure from parents. Parental advocacy, since PL 94-142 was passed, has resulted in the creation of special programs that didn't exist in previous decades. Some of these programs include the gifted and talented program (a special-education curriculum designed for children whose intelligence is significantly above average) and individualized programs for learning-disabled children (who used to be either lumped with developmentally delayed children or not identified as disabled at all). Private schools retain more ability to turn away individual children, but only on the basis of the school's *limitations* (for example, a small private school can argue that it literally does not have room for a separate special-education classroom) or its *purpose* (for example, a Catholic school can turn away children whose parents refuse to let them participate in religious instruction). Public schools must accept any child within the district, regardless of the special needs involved. This principle has been reaffirmed in case after case, regardless of the costs to the school district.

## Information Creates Access

The information revolution hasn't only created jobs—it has also created access. In past decades the parent of a child with unusual special needs often felt very alone, especially in a small town or rural district. Such parents can now band together on the Internet across state boundaries, share information, and push for reforms. Educational research can be (and is) disseminated widely and quickly. All this creates a fertile environment for developing educational strategies. To cite just one example, ten years ago there was one generally accepted approach to treating children diagnosed with attention deficit disorder; now there are half a dozen promising new approaches (see Chapter 6). Whatever your child's difficulties with school, there is every reason to believe help is available.

More than ever, it is now crucial not to let your child's dislike of school destroy his natural zest for learning—there are ways to help. The enthusiasm you help preserve may shape your child's future.

## How This Book Came to Be

I am a child and family therapist specializing in school problems. Because I specialize in this area, I receive many requests for help from parents in my community who have children who just aren't thriving in school. Broward County, where I live and work, is the nation's fifth-largest school district, and my experience within it, as well as my earlier experience with the large Houston (Texas) school district, has prepared me to negotiate with schoolteachers and administrators better than can most parents. But initially I was surprised at how many nice, intelligent, concerned parents were having trouble. A few years back, curious to see how great the need actually was, I sent a small flyer to the school district's office of psychological services, offering a free program called ChildFit for parents who wanted help with their child's school placement. The flyer, which I suggested the district distribute as its staff saw fit, read simply "Does your child hate school? Call this number for help."

The staff mailed the flyer, together with a packet of information on other community services, to area elementary schools. Within a short period of time I was so inundated with referrals that I had to start training my graduate students to help out in the program. Independently of each other, four local elementary schools featured the program in their PTA newsletters. This attracted the attention of local reporters, and the program was then profiled in the *Miami Herald*. From there, the story was picked up by the Associated Press. To date, it has appeared in twenty newspapers nationwide, and more clippings come in every day as newspapers run their back-to-school sections. I have received phone calls from all over the country, with parents offering to fly to Florida for this service or pleading with me to tell them where they can turn for help within their own community.

It's clear to me that there is a great need for this kind of help for parents and that I can reach many more parents through a book. I know how these desperate parents feel—I have personal experience with these issues as well. My daughter is now eleven and an honor roll student classified by the school district as "highly gifted." Back when she was five, however, she nearly flunked out of kindergarten before I managed to get her into the appropriate special program. My knowledge of school systems didn't help me then; I had to learn some new rules about how to make the system work for *my* child. I learned—the hard way! I also have four stepchildren, ranging in age from eleven to twenty-three, and all of them have had school difficulties at one time or another, as do nearly all children. I have shared the rules I learned with my own children through the ChildFit program, and I want to share them now with you.

Because I know what I know from the perspective of an advocate for children and families and from being a parent myself, I wanted someone else to bring in the teacher's perspective. My colleague and cousin, Julie Little, M.S., agreed to help me out. Julie has twenty years' experience in education. She has taught every variety of students, from those in regular classrooms to specialized populations of the severely disturbed emotionally and the profoundly delayed developmentally at the elementary, middle, and high school levels. She earned a master's degree in exceptional-student education. In contrast to my experience in large, urban school districts, Julie has experience in several small, rural districts, as well as in suburban areas. She is presently a consultant to other educators on classroom-behavior management, and she works as a consultant to parents on enhancing their children's organizational skills. Julie has contributed the sections entitled "Teacher Tips," in which she shares with parents helpful strategies for communicating with their children's teachers—and reminds us (as teachers like to do) about what we should be doing at home to back up the school.

## Starting the Journey

As you embark on guiding your child's educational journey, this book can be your road map. I am speaking to you from my position as a passionate advocate for children, as a child and family therapist, and as someone who has had a personal and professional lifetime filled with coaxing schools into meeting the needs of individual, very different children. I encourage you to exercise your rights and get what your child needs, in whatever school setting you choose, and I have drawn on case examples of the parents I have helped to help their children. Julie adds her school "insider's" perspective. As a reminder that failure in school is not failure in life, we also include brief interviews with successful adults who struggled in school as children.

*I Know My Child Can Do Better!* is divided into two parts. Part I, "Getting Started," tells you what you need to know to begin exploring options for your child. Then, Part II, "Finding Your Way," details the five most common reasons why children "hate" school and offers a range of solutions for you to try.

In both sections, at the end of each chapter is a list of resources for you to obtain more information on the topics discussed in that chapter. There are also family activities suggested in each chapter for you to try to make the learning process accessible to and fun for the whole family. My overall goal is to support and empower you. When making decisions about your child's education, if you're given the information, options, and encouragement you need, you as a parent really do know best.

## Family Activity

**T**o further explore the issues raised in the Introduction, here is an interactive activity that the whole family might enjoy. Describe to your children what a typical elementary school day was like for you, and listen to how their experiences have been both different and in some ways similar. Now log onto www.sckans.edu/~orsh, and look at the collection of stories and photographs of one-room schoolhouses throughout the Midwest (less than a hundred years ago) and in rural areas (often less than fifty years ago). How much has education changed in the United States, and when did change become so rapid?

## Resources

Here are resources related to the topics of schools and social change.

## Books

E.D. Hirsch, *The Schools We Need: And Why We Don't Have Them* (New York: Random House, 1999).

Rita Caccamo, *Return to Middletown: Three Generations of Sociological Analysis* (Palo Alto, CA: Stanford University Press, 1999).

David Tyack and Larry Cuban, *Tinkering Towards Utopia: A Century of Public School Reform.* (Boston, MA: Harvard University Press, 1997).

## Websites

The home site of the U.S. Department of Education gives information (www.ed.gov) on general educational trends, especially in the public schools. The home site of the Alternative Education Resource Organization (www.edrev.org) offers both information on and links to a wide variety of independent schooling options. Visit www.smartmarriages.com for links to a research archive on marriage, divorce, and general family statistics. The home site promotes family-life education and is sponsored by the nonprofit Coalition for Marriage, Family, and Couples Education.

# PART I

# Getting Started

In this part we consider what you need to know to be an effective advocate for your child and her education. The first step is to get to know your son or daughter well enough to be able to describe to professionals (who don't know him or her nearly as well as you do) what makes your child unique.

In Chapter 1 we give you some ideas about how to do that. There we also begin to describe how the educational system works, going over the terms and references that can be so confusing when you first hear them, terms such as *magnet*, *charter*, and *alternative*. Then in Chapter 2 we take a deeper look at the school system and its unwritten rules that everyone knows but never talks about.

In this first part, "Getting Started," we are looking at overall patterns and at a wide range of options. In Part II, "Finding Your Way," we discuss specific complaints. For now, let's just take a step back and consider what we know about the system—and what you know about your child.

# 1

# How the System Works

You have decided that you are ready to advocate for your child to get a better education. What do you need to know to get started? Like most journeys, this one begins at home. The first step is to get to truly know your child, well enough to explain to the outside world what is unique about him or her. For most parents, this will mean sitting back and doing some observing.

## Step One: Get to Know Your Child

Picture two young, elementary-school-age girls playing with fashion dolls. At first glance, you might see them both as engaged in the same activity. But a closer look tells you something more about each girl's approach to life. Sarah's doll is off on an adventure—she is piled into a toy car along with several other dolls, and Sarah explains they are off to find buried treasure. Sarah is an imaginative child, quick to explore new things but also easily bored. She tends to take the leadership role in a group. Her friend Kate has contributed her doll to Sarah's trip. Kate is a child who tends to fol-

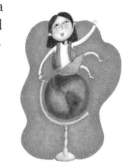

low others' lead in play. She seems a bit confused about what it is the dolls are doing, but is content to let Sarah make up the story. However, periodically Kate does check on and stroke her doll, covering her doll with a tiny blanket, making sure her doll is "rested." Kate had health problems herself as a younger child, and her anxious solicitude toward her doll imitates her parents' care of her. Having observed their play in this detail, it would not be hard to predict which child might get in trouble at school for being too outspoken and which child would unlikely present a behavior problem but might lag somewhat in language skills.

Let me add an example from my consulting practice. Wanda was referred to me after complaining to her son's school guidance counselor about the results of his testing. She felt sure her son must be qualified for a gifted program within his school district, yet the times she had taken him for an intelligence test, he tested within the high-normal range. Sometimes these tests are indeed misleading. But I noticed that Wanda based her expectations on her own and her husband's background of high academic achievement. When I asked what her son is actually like, she described to me an active, outgoing boy who loves sports and is unusually popular among his peers. Academic work is not his primary interest, and may perhaps not be his primary talent. For a moment I found myself wishing Wanda's son could trade places with Liam, the only son of a professional athlete. Liam and his father were scheduled to see me later on so I could help Liam explain to his dad how he was so busy thinking about his science project that he failed to see the ball coming his way and (again) lost the soccer match for his team.

Many times when I ask parents to describe their children, they begin by saying, "Oh, he's just normal," or "She's pretty typical—just like the other ten-year-olds." In a group, children of similar ages can all seem pretty much the same. But if you look more closely, the unique individuality of each child does come through.

It can take an even closer look to separate out what you want your child to be like or what you expect your child to be like, based on what you were like, from the actual child in front of you. Every child is a surprise, a human different from any other individual. It is easy to get so busy admonishing and encouraging children, not to mention keeping them fed, clothed, and healthy, that you may not slow down long enough to just watch them, really observe your children and appreciate the ways in which they are unique. You will be a far more effective advocate for your child if you have a clear picture of what that child is like and can articulate that to others.

Here are some observational exercises to get you started.

## Observe Your Child Playing with Other Children

Sit back and try not to interfere (except in emergencies) as your child plays with others of the same age. Which children take the lead in directing the play? Which children are good team players? Inevitably, there will be conflicts. Notice when they occur whether your child is the youngster who gets too bossy. Is he or she the child who quietly withdraws? Or is your child the mediator, who gets the group back together playing happily? Try to set aside ten or fifteen minutes a week to quietly watch your child out on the playground with other children, and notice any recurring patterns.

## Keep a Small Notebook

Use a notebook for your observations. Write down every time someone outside the family praises or criticizes your child. What others tend to notice, whether positive or negative, may be part of a larger pattern. Remember that criticism and praise frequently are just two sides of the same coin. For example, the talkativeness Sarah's teacher complains about fits in with the great imagination her babysitter praises; the nice manners Kate's teacher praises may go along with the tendency to get bullied on the playground that her day-care worker mentions.

## Notice What Fascinates Your Child

Does your youngster spend hours reading? Is she the neighborhood soccer champion? What are his favorite movies, favorite television shows, and favorite games? What interests do you notice that you share, or that he shares with others in the family? What pursuits are just your child's interests?

## Play a Talking Game with Your Child

Invent scenarios for discussions with your youngster. If there were a disaster and your child had time to save only three items before evacuating the house, what would those three items be? If your child had three magic wishes, what would they be? (No fair wishing for more wishes!) What's the most fun your child ever had, and what made that occasion so much fun? Be prepared to answer the questions yourself as well, so it remains a game and doesn't become an interrogation. And remember there are no right or wrong answers, only a chance to explore your child's thinking.

## Go for a Trip Down Memory Lane

With older children and teens, get out the photo album and reminisce about their early childhood. What do you notice about your fifteen-year-old that is the same as it was when he or she was five? What are the most consistent aspects of your child's approach to the world? To get you started, these are some traits that developmental research has identified as among those most likely to stay constant over time, from infancy to adulthood.

- *Activity level*—Is your child constantly on the go, or a couch potato?
- *Approach time*—Is your child slow to warm up, shy in new situations, or does she jump right in as the life of the party?
- *Temperament*—Is your child basically happy-go-lucky and cheerful? Is he more often serious and thoughtful or reflective?
- *Curiosity*—Is your child content to watch the world go by? Was it your child who had to take the clock apart to see how it worked or explore every cupboard in the house?

See if you can also identify any consistent interests. Many children are interested in puppies and kittens in their preschool years, but if your child went on to be passionate about horses, for example, all through elementary school, and volunteered with Wildlife Rescue in middle school, you have indications of what may be a real lifetime strength.

## Focus on Your Child's Strengths

Every child has talents. Can you identify three particular strengths of your child? Hang onto those positive thoughts— even write them down. They will be invaluable in getting you both through discouraging times. And make sure to share with your child what you notice that makes you proud and happy.

## Step Two: Know Your Options

So now you know that your child enjoys physical activity and gets restless if forced to stay still for too long. Or perhaps your kid reads voraciously to himself, but is shy when reading aloud in a group. What do you do with that information? What options do you have, other than the same school and same teacher as your next-door neighbor's very different child?

In subsequent chapters, we suggest more detailed options for more specific needs. Right now, however, I want to clarify what your options are in general, so you are aware of the whole picture and so that the later suggestions make sense when we come to them.

### *Basic Public School Options*

Public schools are funded by the local school district, primarily through property taxes. For this reason, schools in areas with more expensive homes have tended to be superior, although in recent years there has been pressure for states to equalize public school funding within and even across districts (as in the landmark *Rodriguez v. San Antonio Independent School District* court decision).[1] In response partly to criticism about inequities and to promote desegregation, most districts introduced *magnet schools* within the last twenty years and *charter schools* within the last decade. Within the public school system in most districts, therefore, you as a parent will be choosing from among the following options.

### Neighborhood Schools

The public school appropriate for your child's age group, for which your home address is "zoned," is known as a neighborhood school. This may or may not be the school geographically closest to your home, as school boundary zones are sometimes oddly shaped to maximize diversity or even out student enrollment between institutions. But the neighborhood school is likely to be one not far from your place of residence.

### "Hardship" Schools Near Place of Employment

In most districts, should you be dissatisfied with your neighborhood school, you can apply to transfer to the school closest to your place of employment, another parent's place of employment, or even the place of employment of a grandparent or caretaker who picks up your child after school. This little-known provision is to make transportation easier for parents, but it can also serve to get your child out of one public school and into another that you prefer. If you can prove a particular hardship (for example, that it is difficult for you to make it out to your child's neighborhood school for school events) and argue that another school is more conveniently located for your particular situation, you can provide an acceptable reason for transfer.

### "Magnet" Schools

Magnet schools were initially set up to provide an alternative to busing for desegregating the public schools. At a magnet school, subject matter in all or most classes is related to a particular special interest. For example, at a magnet school for performing arts the students may be asked to put on a play in a history class and to practice their spelling words by writing songs about them, and a local theater group may volunteer time to work with the students. At a magnet school for health professions, the history teacher may cover the history of medicine, and the English teacher may introduce words particular to the health professions during spelling lessons; local physicians, nurses, and technicians often are guest speakers. It is important to note that magnet schools do not necessarily offer a more advanced curriculum, but simply a curriculum that concentrates on a particular interest area.

In the past, admission to magnet schools could be contingent on the particular ethnic and cultural balance the school district was trying to promote within a particular school. Although some school districts still aim for this, court decisions have confirmed that this is unfair to minority students. (Magnet programs are typically placed within an inner-city school, to persuade students from more affluent areas to voluntarily travel across town.) Therefore, if you suspect your child was denied admission to a magnet school because of concerns about ethnic balance, you are within your rights to complain and get the decision overruled. And it generally will be, if only by more highly placed district officials who are familiar with the court cases in question. However, if a magnet program is quite popular, admission may be handled on a first-come, first-served (or even on a lottery) basis, and this is allowable. Regular curriculum may be offered at the magnet school in addition to the magnet program curriculum, especially at the middle and high school levels.

## "Charter" Schools

Charter schools are a more recent innovation of the 1990s, and most developed at the end of that decade. Thirty-six states now have charter schools. In these thirty-six states, parents, teachers, community groups, or other interested parties may open a school by direct contract with the state (a charter), rather than going through a local school district. This allows the organizers of a charter school to offer a specialized program, such as a focus on the fine arts, or an innovative approach to classroom management, without being limited by all the guidelines of the regular public schools within the district. For example, a popular charter school in my area requires parents to volunteer in the classroom and incorporates lessons on "character-building values," such as loyalty and forgiveness, along with its regular curriculum. A traditional public school could not require these things, in case parents of the children there objected. But as charter schools are voluntary—parents choose them as a preference—they have more autonomy.

Charter schools are funded with public money, however, receiving a tuition grant from the state for each public school student who selects the particular charter school. They are therefore banned from collecting tuition from parents, though in other respects they may seem more like private than public schools. There are as many different types of charter schools as there are groups willing to organize them, and the quality ranges from much better than the local public schools to somewhat worse; parents should evaluate each individually, with a view to the needs of their particular child.

### Satellite Schools
Sometimes a museum, university, or other off-campus educational institution is connected with a regular public school. Students at these "satellite" schools have periodic enrichment activities, and may have some actual classes, at the off-campus institution.

The options discussed here, where available, are open to every child within the school district.

## Specialized Public School Options
If you are able to persuade school officials that your child has special needs, your child will come under the provisions of the Individuals with Disabilities Education Act (IDEA). As we dis-

cussed in the Introduction, this federal law has ushered in a quiet revolution in public schools, resulting in parents demanding—and getting—a wide range of individualized, highly specialized services for their children. The word *disabilities* implies to many parents an irreversible condition, such as severe mental retardation, or a visible handicap, such as being confined to a wheelchair. Actually, however, IDEA applies to a wide range of situations, including children who are temporarily experiencing emotional difficulties due to a family transition, "gifted" children who are of above-average intelligence and get bored in regular classes, children who have been diagnosed with attention deficit disorder, and children with specific learning disabilities, including difficulty with writing or reading or an aversion to mathematics. In Part II, under each specific area of difficulty, we will explain when it may be worthwhile to go about getting your child included in an IDEA category—and how to do so. For now, keep in mind that if a change of school is justified, wide-ranging exceptions can and will be made for your child, resulting in an educational experience that is close to being customized.

For your child to be eligible for such an individualized educational plan, you must present "evidence of exceptionality," which will be placed in your child's public school file. What constitutes "evidence" is different for every diagnosis, and this, too, will be discussed in subsequent chapters.

## Private School Options

Private schools are funded by tuition from parents, and, in most instances, are also supported by religious organizations or charitable foundations. They are more independent of the state than are public schools, and so they are also referred to as "independent" schools. To be accredited, private schools have to meet some requirements similar to those of the public schools, such as nondiscrimination clauses and certain education credentials for teachers. Private schools typically fall into one of three categories: religious, preparatory, and alternative.

### Religious Private Schools

There are religious schools for every major faith. The most common type is the parochial or Catholic school, which is found in almost every urban area. A growing category is the "Bible-based" school run by Evangelical Protestants, most common in rural or suburban areas and throughout the South. Jewish and Islamic schools are found primarily in urban areas with larger populations. In using the term *religious school*, in this context I mean a school offering an *entire curriculum*, not simply religious instruction after regular school hours or on weekends.

More conservative religious schools typically have a curriculum described as "back to basics," "Bible-based," or "traditional." Teachers in these schools utilize drill and memorization to a greater degree than do educators in the public schools. In particular, they are likely to stress the "phonics" approach to reading. (The hotly controversial phonics–whole language debate is discussed in Chapter 5.) Religious schools that describe themselves as "academic," "modern," or "progressive" are more likely to resemble a standard preparatory school with religious instruction added. Religious private schools in general do offer certain advantages:

• Tuition is relatively low for private schools, as it is subsidized by the parent religious organization. In cases of need, clergy may also be appealed to for scholarships, and often will intervene to help out if a family is a long-standing member of the particular church, temple, synagogue, or mosque.

- Classes tend to be smaller and discipline is usually stricter. This is especially important for children who lag developmentally or who have easily scattered attention, as will be discussed in subsequent chapters. This feature, in common with the emphasis on drill found in some religious schools, can be a disadvantage for a child who is ahead of schedule developmentally, however, or for the child with nonacademic interests who may feel trapped by the strict format.
- Beliefs and values learned at home can be reinforced at school. This fit between school and home is the primary attraction for most parents who choose a religious school for their children.

Most religious schools accept tuition-paying students of any faith. However, the parents do have to be comfortable with their child's receiving specifically religious instruction. Parents may also be asked to make sure their child conforms in matters of dress, diet, and demeanor to other children who are being raised in the religion. As with other private schools, religious schools may refuse to accept a student whose disabilities cannot be accommodated by the school without having resources beyond its means. Tuition costs vary in religious schools, with scholarships and special arrangements within the faith community not uncommon. Religious schools of all types are common at the elementary school level, but an increasing number now extend grade levels through high school.

### Preparatory Private Schools

Private schools that describe themselves as *preparatory* specialize in academically rigorous preparation for college. Tuition is typically steep, and the atmosphere may be elitist. Class sizes are smaller than in the public schools, with discipline stricter. The level of the curriculum may be geared to high achievers, but at least as often it will target average students who simply learn better with more attention from the teacher and fewer distractions. Preparatory schools are the type of private school most likely to offer a boarding option. This can be useful for teenagers who need to escape from a difficult family situation or negative peer group. (The pros and cons of the "flight" reaction to peer-group trouble will be discussed in Chapter 7.) Preparatory schools seldom focus on drill and memorization, but instead attempt to promote critical thinking and foster extended independent projects as a preparation for college. However, they are still teacher-centered and have traditional classrooms, unlike alternative private schools.

Most preparatory schools will not admit children whose disabilities they are not equipped to handle. Nor will they admit children whose academic records show too many difficulties with behavior or learning. The exceptions are those private preparatory schools marketed specifically to children diagnosed with attention deficit disorder, educational institutions that tend to offer an extra dose of structure. Tuition costs at preparatory schools are typically high, but academic and other scholarships are a possibility. Preparatory schools are most common at the high school level, although they have become increasingly available at the middle and elementary levels as well, especially in larger urban areas.

### "Alternative" Private Schools

Most private schools that call themselves *alternative* follow a particular, defined educational model. (These schools should not be confused with designated "alternative schools" within the public school system, which are usually reserved for children who have behavior problems in the regular classroom.) Most often, the defined educational model at private schools emphasizes greater freedom and exploration than the average public school. Teachers are required to have additional, specific training in the educational model, and are typically quite enthusiastic about it. This is an advantage if the given model works for your child. However, it may be a disadvantage for the child who doesn't fit with the model, who will typically be asked to leave the school—rather than the school's personnel being willing to alter the approach in which they are so steeped.

There are several examples of common alternative schools:

• **Montessori schools,** which follow the model of Maria Montessori, a pioneer in the field of early childhood education. In Montessori schools, the teacher sets up the classroom context and then functions as a facilitator and observer. Children are encouraged to be independent and self-reliant, with even very young children, for example, preparing and serving their own snacks. Children move from learning center to learning center at their own individual pace, but within a structured format. Montessori classrooms tend to be quiet and peaceful, with children learning at their individual paces and moving around at will.

• **Waldorf schools,** which utilize the educational model of Rudolf Steiner, an early educator who rebelled against the rigid schools of his native Austria. Waldorf schools emphasize art, music, and drama as tools for learning. Children are encouraged to develop their "feeling intelligence" through imaginative play. The format is less structured than Montessori, and there is more emphasis on outdoor exercise and moving to music. Teachers actively collaborate with the children on projects, as well as observing and facilitating the children's work. Waldorf classrooms tend to be bustling, creatively messy, and full of small-group activity.

• **Reggio Emilia schools,** which are named after an innovative, late-twentieth-century community school in Italy. In this format, children as a group choose the topics they want to study and carry through a project by teamwork and group planning. There is heavy emphasis on group solidarity and decision making by the learning community. Teachers are both facilitators and members of the group. Classrooms may resemble committee meetings—or everyone may be outside painting a mural.

While these are the most common types of alternative private schools, many communities have one or more schools that follow the unique teaching philosophy of their owners and founders or apply a combination of the above approaches. The National Coalition of Alternative Community Schools can offer a local listing of available schools in your area.[2]

Alternative private schools have these features in common, relative to more traditional schools: a less-structured format; an emphasis on the teacher as collaborator and helper, rather than as authority figure; and a greater use of art, music, drama, and hands-on projects. Thus, they may offer a viable alternative for children with nonacademic interests that coincide with the school's or for academically accelerated children who are self-motivated enough to thrive in this format. On the other hand, they may be a poor fit for children who need more structure or are easily distracted by activity around them.

For children who may have been labeled with a disability or difference, the alternative schools are typically the most open options among the private schools. School officials may also be willing to overlook past behavior or learning problems if the parent argues that an overly traditional format was at fault for a child's poor learning. Tuition costs vary, with parental participation (volunteer work, bartering for services, teaching a skill within the school) usually an option to reduce tuition costs. Alternative schools are most common at the preschool and elementary levels, with middle and high schools available in the larger urban areas.

## Educational Extras: Something on the Side

Whatever school format parents choose, they can also supplement their child's education by hiring a tutor. Tutors provide extra, additional instruction outside school hours. Most often, parents choose this option when they have a child in the public schools who, they feel, needs extra attention and instruction. The extra instruction a tutor provides is typically in an area of study that is especially difficult for the child, although it may incorporate basic study skills as well. This supplement may be quite helpful for a child who is simply a bit behind in school achievement or work and can catch up with extra time and explanation. Yet it can be a recipe for increased frustration for the child with an undiagnosed learning disability or an emotional issue that needs to be addressed. In later chapters we discuss when hiring a tutor is advisable and when it likely would be wasted effort.

If you decide to look for a tutor, a good place to start is at the college or university closest to your home. Check with its undergraduate education department to find future teachers who are interested in working with children individually. Your child's school guidance counselor may also be aware of local tutors, perhaps teachers in the school who moonlight, whom other families have used with success. For a broader set of recommendations, a free service is available on-line that will locate a choice of qualified tutors for you in your area, based on your customized request.[3]

## Home Schooling—the Surprise Alternative

Home schooling is now legal in all fifty states. When I first mention this option to parents, most simply laugh. The picture that springs to their minds is of a rural family, with mother in an apron spending all day, every day, educating her brood at home while father grows the family's food and builds its furniture. This seems remote from urban life, especially now that over 70 percent of women with children work full-time outside the home. However, the tremendous growth in home schooling during the past decade means that, while some home-school families more or less fit this stereotype, many more do not. To dispel the myths, I usually start by telling parents what they are *not* required to do in order to home-school:

• Neither parent has to be home full-time during the day. Education can be provided in the evenings and after what are (arbitrarily, based on outmoded agricultural needs) the usual public school hours. Of course, children too young to be left alone need adult supervision of some kind during the times both parents are away. But there is no requirement for parents to give up outside employment.

• Parents do not have to provide all the teaching themselves. It is perfectly acceptable for parents to hire tutors and college students who are skilled in particular subject areas, trade off with other home-schooling parents, or even hire a moonlighting public school teacher. There are many published curriculums for homeschoolers, complete with workbooks, textbooks, and exams. In addition, there are now complete on-line curriculums, including some with interactive features, so that your child can "converse" via E-mail, even in real time and with a qualified teacher.

• Parents do not have to have teaching degrees. In February 1994 Congress passed legislation making it illegal for states to require specific educational credentials of parents educating their own children. Legally, you are automatically an "expert" when it comes to your own child.

• Parents do not have to go it alone. There are local home-schooling organizations (at least one) in every major city in the United States, and a plethora of home-schooling websites, support groups, and, in most larger cities, "group" times scheduled for homeschoolers at bookstores (story time and special activities), libraries, and museums. Ironically, at times there seems to be more support for homeschoolers than for parents attempting to cope with difficult situations in public schools.

This is not to say that home schooling is the option of choice for every parent—or even for most parents. The undertaking certainly requires considerable commitment. However, it can be a useful option for the self-motivated, academically accelerated child and for the child whose difficulties with attention are exacerbated in a group. More broadly, mentioning the option serves to remind parents that they do have freedom of choice, and need not feel trapped into any one situation. You can walk your child away from any school situation you do not like, at any time, if you are willing to try educating him on your own.

Home schooling can be done at any age, and home-schooled children have been competitive with their peers in gaining college admission. State requirements vary, from the extremely nonrestrictive (a simple declaration of intent by the parent) to the curriculum-based (parents must choose a curriculum approved by the state, typically one of the published or on-line versions but not one the parent invents on the spur of the moment). Children must be tested once a year to determine their progress. In general, the western states tend toward the wholly nonrestrictive, and the eastern states toward the curriculum-based, but there are exceptions. To find the specific requirements for home schooling in your state, log on to www.home-school.com, go to Frequently Asked Questions, and locate the contact persons for your state.[4] Asking these specific home-school contacts is preferable to asking local school-district personnel, who tend to discourage home schooling as a matter of course and who may not be current with the rapidly changing rules in your area.

### Family Activity

**T**o involve the whole family in further exploration, go to www.edrev.org, the home page of the Alternative Education Resource Organization. This site has a truly exhaustive list of alternative options. Discuss and fantasize about these ideas: Did you know you could get a high school degree by correspondence from Australia? Would you want to? What options look appealing, if perhaps unworkable? Which options simply look strange to you?

## Step Three: Know Your Rights

As a parent, you have the right to see your child's school records and to receive a copy of anything and everything that is in your child's file. If your child attends public school, you have the right to insist on testing for any specific disability you suspect (or for giftedness). Of course, the school in turn has the right to put you on a waiting list. For now, be aware that testing does *not* have to be initiated by the school or requested by the teacher (in later chapters we will discuss specific strategies you can use). You have the right to meet with any and all of your child's teachers. Should your child be identified as having a disability of some kind, a private school cannot turn that child away without demonstrating that it is truly impossible for it to meet the youngster's needs. A public school cannot turn the child away at all, and is mandated to provide an optimal, individualized education that meets the child's special needs.

You have the right to withdraw your child from any school, public or private, at any time and to educate the child in a manner of your own choosing (which may include keeping the child at home). Contrary to what you may hear from dismayed school officials, this does not constitute "truancy" if you are in the process of developing (or even considering) a viable plan for home schooling. You also have the right to decide to quit home schooling your child, and to return him or her to the public school system, at any time. While you can't go back and forth with this too often without confusing the child and annoying the school, it is good to know no decision is irrevocable.

Most of all, you have the right to feel you are truly directing your child's education, choosing the path that will eventually—and optimally—lead your child from the embrace of early childhood into the adult world. To do this well, however, you also need to be aware of the underlying assumptions common to our school system, the "unwritten rules" of school success, which are covered in the next chapter.

Before moving on to Chapter 2, though, take a moment and review our first set of "Teacher Tips." These tips from a teacher's perspective will help you consider what you can do at home to help your child, providing a more solid foundation before you move on to make changes elsewhere.

## TEACHER TIPS

Your child should see you and his or her teachers as *partners* in a common cause. This attitude of partnership smooths the transition from home to school, and back again. Whatever the child's other difficulties with school, it can't hurt (and might well help) to begin by reinforcing the idea of that basic partnership. Here are some questions to consider.

**Do You Respect Your Child's School Commitments?**
During the school years, parents must accommodate the schedule the child's education demands. This means keeping the whole household to a reasonable weekday sleep schedule, minimizing vacations during the school year, and making necessary appointments for the child outside of school hours. It may also mean planning dinner and evening activities around the child's need to have time for both relaxation and homework. Sports and other extracurricular activities are important—but school is (or should be!) more important.

**Does Your Child See You Helping Out at School?**
Nothing sends a more powerful message to a child about the importance of school than the sight of parent and teacher working together. This is not an option limited to parents who are full-time homemakers. Many employers allow an employee to volunteer an hour or two a month during school hours. If this volunteer work is not possible, try letting your child see you purchase art supplies, reward stickers, or extra pencils to be given to the teacher (and you can do this even when you do volunteer time at school). Although most teachers in fact spend a considerable amount of their own money on such supplies, the point is not the monetary value—but the gift from parent to teacher to support the teacher's classroom efforts. Such spontaneous gifts should not be presented as coming from 7the child, but as coming from the parent, as one colleague to another. Similarly, when you cut out a newspaper or magazine article, commenting that it might interest Teacher X, your child gets the point that you and Teacher X com-

municate and share mutual interests. As one eight-year-old child commented wisely to another, "When you see your Mom and your teacher talking to each other and smiling about it, you kind of remember all the grown-ups are on the same side."

### Do You Keep Open the Lines of Communication?

Read your child's homework assignments, school memos, and anything else that comes home from school. Ask questions and make comments. Since your child's classroom teacher ordinarily cannot talk to you during school hours, send in a note or leave a phone message, with a phone number where the teacher can reach you after hours. If you have sent in two or more notes and your child's teacher has not responded, contact the school guidance counselor for help in setting up a meeting. Don't go over the teacher's head to the principal or over the principal's head to the district office until you have first tried the teacher and guidance counselor. The guidance counselor is a support to the classroom teacher, but the principal is the teacher's supervisor (as the district administrator is the principal's). Most people, teachers included, are considerably more defensive when they first hear about a complaint from their boss.

### What Does Your Child Notice You Saying and Doing?

Children are more strongly influenced by their parents than by anyone else, and you are more of an influence than you may realize. If your child hears you complain about his school or teacher, he is likely to agree with you. If your child hears you say that what he is doing in school is a waste of time, he is likely to find it so. Even when you have your differences with teachers and school officials, try to speak positively about them.

The only stronger influence than what your child hears you say is what your child sees you do. Parents try all kinds of punishments and rewards to get their children to read. But the strongest message you can send is simply to turn off the television and let your child see you instead pick up a good book. When you're swamped with work, let your child see you doing paperwork at home, perhaps right alongside his homework, instead of shooing him away. Let your youngster get the message that adults read, work, and learn new things, just as do children in school.

You want what is best for your child and you are absolutely right to fight for your child's needs. Give us teachers a chance, and most of us will show you we are on the same side.

## Resources

Here are additional resources related to the topics we have discussed in Chapter 1.

For more information about *Rodriguez v. SAISD* and the Supreme Court case it spawned, or for more about court decisions in general that have affected the school system, see Peter Irons and Stephanie Guitton, *May It Please the Court* (NY: New York Press, 1993).

To locate the public and private schools available in your area, look in your local telephone directory, in the Yellow Pages for private schools and most often in the regular directory (business) pages for public schools. Another alternative is www.web crawler.com/education/k_12, an on-line school-locator service.

To learn more about particular types of schools, visit these websites:

- For charter schools: www.uscharterschools.org

- For alternative schools: http://ncacs.org

- For another perspective on the public schools: www.pta.org

- For another perspective on home schooling, see Jon's Homeschool Resource Page: www.midnightbeach.com

- For federal educational research and policy, see the Department of Education home page: www.ed.gov

# 2

# The Unwritten Rules
## *How the System* Really *Works*

Certain common assumptions underlie our school system—
although these are not spelled out for parents or for anyone else. Such assumptions "go without saying." Yet at times
they don't. Without knowing these assumptions, parents who
come from a "different" family or cultural background, who
did not themselves do well in school, who had primarily
nonacademic interests, or who simply have not kept up with
how the system has changed over time will be at a great disadvantage—as will their children. Indeed, any of us could use
a reminder of the unspoken, unwritten rules that govern school
performance and evaluation. So let's take a look at the six most
important of these unspoken rules. Most likely, your child's
teacher will not spell these out for you.

## The Squeaky Wheel Gets the Grease

The more services you request, the
more services your child will receive.
The more you call your child to the

school's attention, the better education your child will receive. Parents often assume that the opposite is true—that parents should not "make trouble," ask for special favors, or otherwise call attention to themselves for fear of retribution against their child. In earlier times, particularly in rural areas, it was not considered polite to ask for special treatment or to make appointments with school personnel on behalf of one's child. Those days are long gone. Today, both public and private schools work very much on the "consumer" model, especially in the United States but to a lesser degree in Canada and Western Europe as well. Parents who ask for meetings with school officials are seen as being involved with and concerned about their children's education.

If your child has special needs, more often than not these needs can be accommodated. But if you don't ask, no one will volunteer that. To cite just one example from my practice, I have recently been working with a parent who wishes to enroll her child in Florida's on-line high school program. However, she cannot afford a home computer. The child has been trying, with some frustration, to use the computers at the public library. Finally the parent, just in passing, mentioned to a district official that she wished her child could have a home computer. The official promptly told her about a program under which her child could qualify for that very thing. To her (and my) amazement, she had a new computer within a week. Why had no one ever mentioned this program before? You guessed it—because she had never asked. Not every problem, of course, will get solved so easily. But no problem will get solved if you don't make your needs known. Advocate for your child—ask. Keep asking, politely but firmly, even when you first hear "No"; more often than not, the doors you want to open will open. Timidity, a polite disinclination to ask for special favors, and a fear of seeming pushy, while very understandable or even praiseworthy in other contexts, are not in your best interests when you are advocating for your child.

# The System Isn't Fair

It is a deeply cherished American belief that education makes it possible for the most capable and talented individuals to rise to the top, regardless of family background or income level. Sometimes this works—sometimes it doesn't. In order to have a better chance of making it work for your child, keep in mind some common pitfalls.

## *Rigid Gender Expectations*

If you have a bossy, aggressive, outspoken little girl or a quiet, timid little boy, your child is at risk. Teachers, particularly in the elementary and middle school grades, tend to punish behavior they view as aberrant. Until it is called to their attention, for example, most middle school teachers (and coaches and administrators) do not even realize that they are generally more punitive with girls who speak out of turn than with boys. It genuinely seems to them that the aggressive girl is somehow "causing more trouble" than the aggressive boy, even when both children are doing exactly the same thing. If this is your child's situation, you will need to be extra vigilant to make sure your child is not penalized for not conforming to common cultural stereotypes.

## *Low Overall Expectations*

Learning disabilities are more likely to go undiagnosed in poor children and children of color. If Johnny is the only son of a wealthy family and both his parents have college degrees, it is of major concern when he isn't learning to read. If Johnny is one of six children born to a single mother living below the poverty line, however, some teacher or administrator is all too likely to say, "Well, what really do you expect?" In part this discrepancy is related to the squeaky-wheel rule we just discussed. Parents with the time, energy, and self-confidence to complain do get more results, especially if they play golf with the district superintendent or work with the principal's spouse. But there is an insidious element to these perceptions that goes beyond this factor. All too often, the low expectations get communicated to the child. To guard against this, if your child is of a minority ethnic group, speaks English with an accent, or for any other reason might be viewed by some teachers in terms of their own limiting stereotypes, be especially vigilant to be an advocate:

- Speak up and complain when warranted.
- Monitor what other children the age of your child are learning. Check out the children of relatives, other children in your church or temple, and children at schools across town, not just other children in your child's class. If you see that your child's development or achievement is behind, don't accept soothing advice "not to worry."
- Volunteer at your child's school and make other efforts to bring in adult role models of the same cultural background as your child (especially if teachers and administrators are not part of this group).
- If you as the parent are treated with disrespect, consider having your child change schools. I once worked with a concerned single mother whose seven-year-old boy was doing poorly in school. At the mother's request, the school psychologist tested the child, finding that there was nothing wrong

other than what she described as "poor behavior." After sharing the results of the testing with the mother, however, the psychologist shut the report back up in her notebook. Assuming this was merely an oversight, I reminded the psychologist that, *by law*, parents must be provided a copy of their children's testing results. Sighing, the psychologist turned to the mother and said in an elaborately slow and patient voice, "I guess I have to give you this copy, but remember, this is a very important document. Be careful not to lose it, even though you won't understand what it says." I was aghast—especially since it happened that this mother handled sensitive legal documents every day at her place of employment. Even aside from that, the fact that the teacher, principal, and counselor all heard the psychologist's admonition to the parent and saw nothing amiss in her patronizing words and tone spoke volumes about the negative climate of low expectations in this particular school. Some schools, sadly, are beyond hope. After consulting with me and sharing her anger about how she had been treated, this child's mother promptly transferred him to another school across town, closer to her place of employment. He gained a grade level in less than a month, no doubt because of his being in a new, more positive school climate. If school officials treat you in a way you cannot feel comfortable with, and do not listen to your attempts to talk with them about this, it is reasonable to conclude that what happens when no parents are around is still worse.

## Evaluations Are Imperfect

Don't assume that your child's grades and scores on standardized tests give a complete and accurate picture of your child's potential. Many contextual factors, apart from the child's natural ability, come into play. A positive relationship with the teacher, helped along by good social skills and classroom behavior, will have a positive effect on a child's grades. This is fair enough—these are quite useful life skills, after all—but it also means that if your child is bored, restless, not getting along with a particular teacher, or out of place in a particular school, his grades may be lower than his ability warrants.

Some bored and restless children respond well to the excitement (and the computer-graded format) of standardized testing. But keep in mind that standardized testing tends to reward verbal skills, even on the mathematical sections of the test. (Figuring out what kind of answer the examiners want is, after all, primarily a verbal skill.) If your child has an easy facility with language, this is good news. But if this is not your child's strength, test scores may come out lower than would be justified by a fairer assessment of your child's overall potential. Being tired, having a cold, or being nervous on the day the test is given are other factors that can affect the outcome.

Familiarity with the language spoken by teachers and examiners is helpful both for grades and for scores on standardized tests. Children for whom English is a second language and children who are not from middle-class homes can be at an unfair disadvantage for this reason.[1] Not only are classroom and test instructions typically given in English, but most often these directions are also in a somewhat verbose English, one that could be called the "dialect" of American middle-class homes. Repeated studies in the field of child development have shown that in situations where a working class or recent immigrant mother would simply say "Hush" to her child, most American middle-class mothers will go on and on: "If I've told you once, I've told you a thousand times, don't interrupt me while I'm on the telephone, because. . . ." This is not necessarily better parenting, but it does build vocabulary. And it is the language style of both the classroom teacher and the written exam. Children unfamiliar with talkative adults who give them long strings of instructions may be at a loss.

Of course, children with undiagnosed learning disabilities may do well at times and not at other times, depending on how the material is presented. We will discuss the language effect and the possibility of learning disabilities at greater depth in Part II. For now, we simply want to make the point that since all tests or measures are partial and dependent on context, you should not accept any one number (whether grade point average, I.Q. score, or another type of test score) as a full and accurate measure of your child's ability.

## Most Parents Help Their Kids Compete

Now this is definitely not one you will have an easy time getting teachers and school officials to say out loud. But the reality is that middle-class parents routinely boost their children's work, and teachers expect that they will do so. Just the opposite is the usual overt message. Parents are routinely told they should never do their children's homework for them, and should expect the child to complete all assignments independently. They are also encouraged to cooperate with other parents, and certainly not to compare their children's work with other children's in a competitive manner.

But a quick glance at the projects turned in for the science fair at the average suburban elementary school makes plain that another message lies just under the surface. The hapless child whose parents really did let her do the science project "all by herself" will be graded down in comparison to the many children whose typed reports and architecturally drafted posters make clear their parents' extensive involvement. While this is less true of everyday homework and class work, it still holds. It is still the case that the child whose parent checks over his work, provides special materials not on the required list (colored pencils instead of crayons for the art project, laser-printed instead of handwritten papers, shiny new folders for reports), and makes extra trips to the library and museum will be at an advantage. And the volume of homework most teachers assign requires that a parent add support, encouragement, and explanations as an active partner in the homework process. Talk to middle-class mothers with children in elementary school, and you will hear a lot of plural pronouns: "We haven't started on our book review yet," "We need to work harder on our math homework this year," and so on. Sometimes it is not clear who is more invested in a particular project, the child or the parent.

We are not suggesting that you must become so overly involved. But we are suggesting that you not assume your child can complete every assignment without your participation. While the work should be primarily your child's, of course, it is a reality that most of the time, especially in the lower grades, you are assumed to be involved as well. Don't let your child be the only one to show up with a magnet and a nail, when all the other children are wheeling in huge science projects that were created as a family collaboration.

On the other hand, speak out when you conclude that more parental involvement is being assumed than your family can handle. The U.S. Department of Education suggests twenty minutes of homework for grades one through three, up to forty minutes a day for grades four through six, and up to two hours a day for grades seven through twelve.[2] If your child is being assigned significantly more homework than this guideline on a regular basis, or if she is being assigned so many projects requiring extensive research that every weekend is spent at the library, it may be time to revisit the squeaky-wheel rule.

## Relationships Matter

It is difficult to overstate how much relationships matter at every level. The truism "It's not what you know, it's who you know" may sound cynical. But if we restate it as "People matter more than subject matter," the old saw begins to seem more like the basic reality that it is.

---

### Family Activity

What are the "unwritten rules" at your house about how school projects get done? Have fun with this concept, and make it clear the conversation is safe; nobody will get punished for saying how he thinks things really work. Try asking what a family member notices about the relationship between two other people: for example, ask little sister what she notices about how Mom and big brother handle his science-fair projects. If you keep it light, this family activity can result in some interesting anecdotes and a chance to see yourself as others see you.

---

### *Your Relationship with Teachers*

The parent who goes to the back-to-school night, sends notes frequently to the teachers (and replies to theirs), volunteers to help out in the cafeteria, and shows up at the classroom holiday party gets more attention and respect from his children's teachers. This is unfair. Another parent may be equally devoted to her child, but have less available time or a more inflexible work schedule. But, even though it's unfair, it is the way it works. You will optimize your child's educational opportunities if you nurture relationships with her teachers. This need not take a lot of your time—a few positive notes praising the teacher's efforts or mentioning how much your child enjoyed a particular activity will go a long way to improving your relationship.

## Your Child's Relationships with Teachers

Your child will learn more if he is genuinely attached to his teachers. Do what you can to encourage this relationship. One thing that helps is to relay praise back and forth, in the time-honored tradition of European matchmakers, even when you have to tweak your quotations a bit. When Mrs. Jones reports, "It's a shame to see a child as bright as Johnny wasting so much time in class," even though you do want to address the time management issue at some point, be sure to tell Johnny right away, "Mrs. Jones said she thinks you're bright." Similarly, when Johnny admits, "Well, Tuesday's class wasn't near as boring as usual—the old trout must have read a book," you can translate that into, "Mrs. Jones, Johnny told me he was so interested by that creative special activity you did last Tuesday." My great grandmother used to tell me, "Talk nice. Honey catches more flies than vinegar." This is never truer than when you are facilitating relationships between your child and his teachers.

## Your Relationship, Most Importantly, with Your Child

Your child needs plenty of love and encouragement as he moves from early childhood into the world of school, and from there into the outside world. Renowned child-development expert Urie Bronfenbrenner states that the first and most critical requirement for optimal human development is "one or more persons with whom the child develops a strong, mutual, irrational, emotional attachment." Or, as he has more colloquially expressed it, "Every child needs someone who is crazy about that child."

Too often I see parents in therapy who are losing that bond with their child, perhaps because of the very school problems they are trying to solve. My hope is that the suggestions in this book will prevent some frustrated parents from the parenting equivalent of destroying the village in order to save it.

School is very important, as is achievement in the outside world, and parents are certainly wise to set both clear limits and reasonably high expectations for how their children behave in school. For most children, these expectations mean getting A's and B's on elementary school report cards, when perceived effort still counts for a good deal, and no more than a few C's added to that mix in middle and high school, to allow for the occasional courses that may be genuinely difficult for your child. Some children will do better, and some children will have more of a struggle. But we are certainly not suggesting that you remain calm about D's and F's, about frequent trips to the principal's office for unruly behavior, or about your child's obvious dislike of school.

In your concern, be sure to focus on what can be done to help. Children don't want to fail in school, and bad attitudes aren't hatched overnight. When there are problems, most often there are some changes everyone can make—parent and teacher as well as child. Examining all the options and coming up with a plan will be more productive than simply getting angry, and infinitely more productive than becoming sarcastic with or belittling your child.

## When Did I Last Do Something Fun with My Child?

If school problems have become the focus of your relationship with your child, ask yourself this question. Regular, mutually rewarding "together" time is what binds parents and children. It is a myth that teenagers stop wanting this. Countless times in family therapy a parent has told me something like, "Well, I used to enjoy going fishing with my daughter, but now that she's a teenager she doesn't want to do that any more." Meanwhile the teenager, interviewed separately, complains bitterly, "My mother just doesn't like me any more—we used to go fishing all the time, but now she never takes me."

What actually seems to happen is that in the early teen years, the child becomes shy about asking for time with the parent—afraid of seeming "immature," perhaps even mildly protesting the idea when it's brought up—but secretly still wants and needs the together time. The parent, afraid of seeming too demanding, just drops the idea. And both parent and child feel hurt and lonely. Let me encourage you to persevere—your older child needs time with you just as much as, maybe even more than, your younger ones.

Similarly, children who are struggling in school and are discouraged about their dismal performance need even more together-time, not less, even when they don't know how to ask for it. By all means get the school problem solved, but in the meantime, while you and the child are working on solving the problem, continue to cherish your relationship with each other. That infuriating child whose grades have dropped for reasons you don't understand is still also the same delightful child who can beat you at gin rummy or draw world-class refrigerator art for you. Courses and even whole grades in school can be made up. If you and your child forget the things you like about each other, it will be much harder to get that back.

## Do You Praise More Often than You Criticize?

Research into the causes of divorce has definitively shown that in marriages that endure the spouses make at least five positive comments for every critical one. Divorce is wrenching, but getting emotionally divorced from your child is even worse. Children need to hear those positives, too. If you have been worried about your child's school failures, or pushing hard for continued successes, when was the last time you said something positive to your child? And how many negative comments followed up that positive one?

Sometimes parents get concerned that they are overdoing it. Keep the praise honest—don't say you're pleased with something you don't find pleasing. And keep it focused on effort— praise the hard work that went into writing the extra-credit report, rather than praising the resulting grade (since hard work is under your child's control, unlike a grade, which is not entirely up to the child). Ask yourself if you ever felt your own parents praised you "too much." I ask this question of parents frequently, and I have yet to meet a parent who didn't answer with considerable passion that they could have used more praise, rather than less. Sometimes, as adults, we forget how deeply encouraging and important a parent's genuine approval of some small action or project can be. If you honestly cannot think of anything commendable that your child is doing, outside or inside school, then it may be time to think about some relationship mending. A few sessions with a family therapist could be of great benefit to you all.[3]

Once you have re-cemented all these important relationships, you are ready to move on to the final unwritten rule, which comes to us from Julie, our teacher consultant.

## Your Child Will Drown in Paper if You Don't Help

Without active parental intervention, virtually all elementary school children, and many middle and high school youths, will be completely unable to manage the flow of information from school to home and back again.

Think for a moment about what all is involved. In one day, a child can easily have ten items to take home (a memo to all parents, a note from the teacher, an assignment sheet for a long-term project, a permission slip, two homework worksheets, and four graded papers, let's say). And four of these must be returned to school the next day (a note back to the teacher, the signed permission slip, and the completed homework). The ten items get thrown into a backpack that also contains textbooks, pencils, markers, notebooks, loose paper, leftover lunch money, electronic gadgets, and all the miscellaneous items that accumulate in a child's backpack (an extra pair of socks, a friend's scribbled phone number, a melting candy bar). Now envision all this clutter multiplied by five days a week, thirty-eight weeks a year. Is it really any wonder when the assignment sheet is finally found the day *after* the project is due, or when the homework arrives with mysterious chocolate stains on it?

## TEACHER TIPS

Only a fortunate few are born organized—the rest of us need to learn how to manage. A teacher doesn't have time to teach your child how to be neat or to clean out his backpack—not when she has thirty other children who also need her attention. You are the one elected for this job. The good news is that if you follow these simple tips, you should find your own stress level reduced (as well as your child's and his teacher's).

**Buy Big**
For your elementary school child, invest in a large backpack that can be wheeled. Buy luggage quality if you can possibly afford it, to avoid broken zippers and bulging seams. Encourage your child to regard this as his mobile office. In this way, the child can take home most or all of his books every day, along with necessary papers and materials. This helps you to avoid both a hopelessly cluttered desk at school (better the child should take everything home and deal with it there) and frequent homework lapses ("I can't do my homework because I forgot that book"). The wheels are to prevent back and shoulder strain.

Middle and high school children may rebel against wheeling around such a clunky vehicle. By age twelve, girls tend to prefer messenger-type bags, and boys like the sleeker, hiking-style backpacks. This makes a good bargaining tool with your older child. ("Keep those grades up, and you can carry the leopard-print shoulder bag instead of wheeling in with Old Clunker.") But if you start hearing "I can't study because I forgot my history book" more than once or twice, it may be time to dust off the old office on wheels.

### Institute a Daily Backpack-Unpacking Ritual

This should be pleasant, not punitive. Sit down with your child and his backpack after school or day care and sort through all the contents. Do this *every day*, barring a nuclear disaster. With a younger child, you will be sorting while he helps; with your middle or high school child, he can sort while you help. (However, I know at least one corporate attorney whose secretary sits him down to unpack his briefcase with her every day.) Fix a snack for both of you, if you like, and use the time to chat about your day and your child's day. But keep sorting.

Together, sort everything into one of six piles: trash (the memo you already read, the melting candy bar); supplies (pencils, papers, and so on—take this opportunity to replenish supplies and sharpen pencils); books (text and library—check when those library books are due); things to keep (graded papers and test results); long-term assignments (instructions for the book report due a month from now, information about upcoming events); and short-term assignments (homework due the next day, permission slips). The trash goes into the garbage (or recycling) container; the supplies and books (freshened up) go back in the backpack; and the things to keep go to the parent, who stashes them in some designated location, perhaps a drawer or trunk. That leaves us with the long- and short-term assignments. And for these, we need folders.

### Designate a Folder That Returns to School

Place completed homework, permission slips, and everything else that should go back to school the next day in this folder. The child can do this at bedtime (but you should check on this folder in the early grades).

These days, many children start using a daily planner as early as elementary school. The planner should go in or near this folder. If you put a few blank Post-it notes on top of the planner, your forgetful child can jot down information more quickly, even if he doesn't have the planner open to the right day at the appropriate time. The information on the notes can always be copied into the right section of the planner later on or placed in the goes-back-to-school folder.

**Keep a Second Folder at Home**
Long-term projects go here. Assignment sheets for reports due later, information about upcoming field trips, anything that doesn't need to go back to school tomorrow but that the child will need in the future stays in this folder for future reference.

**In Conclusion**
Sometimes parents object to these recommendations, on the grounds that staying organized should be the child's responsibility. But this is one area where the sink-or-swim model seldom works. If you institute these patterns when your child is seven, you will have a more organized seventeen-year-old than another parent who instead simply elects to spend the intervening decade yelling about irresponsibility. Let your child learn from your peaceful example.

Sometimes it's the older child who objects, on the grounds that unpacking his backpack with you violates his right to privacy. Kids don't have a blanket right to privacy, not as long as they are living under their parents' roof. But certainly you do not want to use the backpack unpacking as a time to needlessly poke and pry. This is meant to be a pleasant, relaxing unwinding from the school day. Just remind your child that a school backpack is for work purposes. Any fledgling love letters can be hidden in pockets or purse. A journal or diary that's intensely personal shouldn't be going back and forth to school anyway. (Remind them that any teacher or school official can open a backpack as well.) And anything bigger than a love letter or a diary that your child wants to hide in his backpack is probably against school rules. Even grown-ups don't get to pack Frisbees in their briefcases (usually), and your child has no inalienable right to do so, either. I hope we are just talking about Frisbees, and not about illegal drugs or weapons. If there are illegal items in your child's backpack, however, you as a parent have both the right and responsibility to find out about that. Our recommendation, on all sides, is to open up that backpack and let the sun shine in.

## Resources

To explore the role of parental involvement in children's school success and the unspoken level of expectation of such involvement, read these two books:

Sharon Ramey and Craig Ramey, *Going to School: How to Help Your Child Succeed* (New York: Goddard Press, 1999).

Dorothy Rich, *Megaskills: How Families Can Help Children Succeed in School and Beyond* (Boston: Houghton-Mifflin, 1992).

For more specifics on how to help the household run smoothly during the school years, see Lee Canter and Lee Hauser, *Homework Without Tears* (New York: Perennial Library, 1987). For organizational tips and strategies that have worked for other parents, log on to www.parentsplace.com/family/organization.

For project ideas in science and social studies, look up www.sci fair.org.

For more general help with homework, www.ajkids.com lets children ask Jeeves, the friendly butler, to find them information.

# II

# Finding Your Way

In this part we get into more specific remedies for given situations. Before we start, though, a few caveats are in order. First, these chapters should not be read as mutually exclusive categories. It is quite possible that your child at times is behind in some areas, accelerated in others, becomes confused, learns differently from some other children, gets inattentive, and also goes through unhappy periods. That could well describe all children! Our reason for dividing the chapters in this way was not to imply that your child must have one type of problem or issue only. There is a finite number of common solutions, however, and these categories allow us to group together similar types of solutions, those that have been useful for many children.

In addition, the school system itself tends to group children in terms of diagnosis, as do many associated professionals. For example, if your child is considered to have attention deficit disorder, certain kinds of remedies will be proposed to you, quite different from the ones that will be suggested if your child is considered to have a learning disability. You may or may not decide it is in your child's best interest to accept whatever label is offered, but it is only fair for us to inform you what label is likely to be offered, given your child's most compelling behaviors, and what the consequences of that label may be.

So the following five chapters each focus on a common set of behaviors, with similar solutions, that are likely to lead to a particular type of diagnosis if that option is pursued. Chapter 3 focuses on children who complain, "It's too hard!" These are the delayed kids, whom teachers may describe as underachieving, unmotivated, or behind schedule. We discuss the possibilities that these individuals are developmentally unready; motivated in a more external or relational way; or interested in areas that are not traditionally considered academic. Consider, however, that the growth-management director of a large city remembers back to his days of being labeled "a slow learner."

Chapter 4 considers children who frequently say, "It's boring!" These are the accelerated youngsters, whom teachers often describe as demanding or impatient. In this chapter we discuss why some children are ahead of schedule in their learning, and the pros and cons of a formal diagnosis of "gifted" (considered by most districts as if it were a disability). As an example, a successful chef recalls the impatience he felt in school.

Chapter 5 considers children who cry, "This is so frustrating!" These are confused youngsters, whom teachers may insist can do the work "when they try." Some of these children may have learning problems and their school performances may be inconsistent. We discuss different teaching approaches, different learning styles, and the role of assistive technology for working with them. The pros and cons of a formal diagnosis of "learning disabled" are also considered. A homemaker explains why she felt she had to give up the idea of becoming a nurse, and what a difference a diagnosis would have made in her situation.

Chapter 6 focuses on kids who explain, "I can't concentrate!" These are the inattentive children, whom teachers may describe as overwhelmed, all over the map, or not on task.

This cluster of behaviors takes us into the controversial area of the attention deficit disorder diagnosis. A wide range of options are discussed, from the traditional to the less common. And a young "dot.com" magnate discusses his attention deficit disorder diagnosis, and his reaction to it.

In Chapter 7, we consider youngsters who complain, "Everybody hates me!" These are unhappy children, whom teachers may describe as being oversensitive or preoccupied, or it may be that the problem is their relationship with the teacher and how they are perceived. We discuss problems with peers, with teachers, and at home. In this chapter, we ask you to remember back to your own unhappy times in school, and provide empathy exercises to help you do this.

Before proceeding to more detailed observations of your child's school difficulties, and to trying new solutions, it would be a good idea to take your child for a physical checkup. Children are more robust and energetic than adults, even when they are ill, and it is possible that what seems like a school problem is really just the lingering effect of symptoms from an infection or other health difficulty. A child who has had a head injury; who appears to be unaware at times that time is passing (and therefore unable to remember what has just happened); who has tics or uncontrollable body movements; or who has difficulty engaging in meaningful conversations with others, may need to be seen by a neurologist as well—discuss this with your pediatrician or family doctor. (For instance, petit mal epilepsy, Tourette's syndrome, and Asperger's syndrome are neurological conditions sometimes mistaken for learning or behavior difficulties. These conditions are beyond the scope of this book, and should be discussed, if warranted, with a qualified medical professional.)

# 3

# "It's Too Hard!"

## *The Delayed Child*

Ed is a conscientious, concerned parent. He has tried to do everything right to help his son in school. That's why it's such a shame that everything he has tried seems to have only made things worse. Ed's son is somehow perpetually "a day late and a dollar short" when it comes to school.

Ed had such high hopes for Teddy, his first child and only son. From the beginning, he took an active role in Teddy's education. When the local public school would not accept Teddy in kindergarten, because he did not turn age five until October, Ed sent Teddy to a private school to get a head start. Then Teddy started first grade when he was five years, eleven months old. Both his kindergarten and first-grade teachers complained that Teddy was rough and boisterous, and had trouble settling down to his work. But he was only a little behind the other students academically, so Ed figured he would grow out of it. In the middle of second grade Teddy did learn to read, and his behavior settled down somewhat. But Teddy continued to have trouble completing his schoolwork by the time the other children had finished theirs, and he

made mostly B's with an occasional C instead of A's with an occasional B, as Ed expected.

Ed began to wonder if the problem was motivation. So he made a deal with Teddy. For every A Teddy received, he would get five dollars to spend as he liked. For a while, Teddy actually seemed to work harder in school, and his teachers reported some improvement. But as time went on, Teddy started to complain that five dollars wasn't a lot of money, that his schoolwork was difficult, and that he wanted bigger rewards. Now, in Teddy's first year of middle school, Ed has promised him an expensive new video-game console and games to go with it if he can keep his grades up to a B average. But Ed is beginning to wonder where all this will end—what will motivate Teddy for next year? Ed feels resentful at the way he finds himself "bribing" Teddy for every little effort.

Meanwhile, Teddy grows more and more disinterested in school. His grades and attitude declined markedly when he entered middle school. Back in elementary school, he kept in touch with his third-grade teacher even in grades 4 and 5, stopping by her classroom after school and showing her the work he was doing. But in his big, busy middle school, Teddy hasn't become acquainted with any teacher that well. In his classes, Teddy is drifting most of the time, trying to figure out how to get by with the minimum effort. He has a C average, and his teachers complain about his lack of effort.

In one area of his life, though, Teddy is right on top of things. At first, back in kindergarten and first grade, Teddy's roughness and awkwardness led to other children avoiding him. But he learned social skills and got to be good at making friends. Now he is the one who keeps in touch with all his old friends from elementary school. He is the leader of his social circle, planning when and where the group will get together next. His teachers complain he spends too much time in school "socializing." At home the telephone rings constantly—and it's nearly always for Teddy. This infuriates Ed. "You're in school to get an education, not to party!" he shouts at Teddy. "Nobody's going to hire you because you're Mr. Popular. You have to buckle down and study if you're going to get a good job one day!" Teddy ignores these lectures. The other day Ed became so frustrated he disconnected the telephone, telling Teddy he was "grounded" until his grades improved.

Now Ed is wondering if the real problem is Teddy's maturity. Maybe he should have listened to Teddy's first-grade teacher, who wanted him to repeat first grade. Maybe if Teddy had been held back in school, he wouldn't be perpetually running behind now. But is it too late now? And what can Ed do to block Teddy's interest in his friends?

"Teddy" is a composite of many children who frustrate their parents because they don't seem to be "on track" in school. There is no one cause for this, and no simple solution, at least after kindergarten. But there are approaches that can help such children enjoy learning and find their own best pace.

Teddy has the following challenges:

• **Developmental lag.** Research shows that children, like Teddy, who start first grade before age six or soon after turning six do not do as well as other children who wait to start until they are older.[1] This is especially true for boys, who develop more slowly than girls throughout the elementary grades. When to start your child in school, when an extra year of kindergarten is warranted, and when repeating a grade can be useful are issues we will discuss in the "Developmental Readiness" section of this chapter.

• **Confused motivation.** With the best intentions in the world, Ed has unfortunately overdone the reward system. He has unwittingly conveyed to Teddy that the boy's achievements are for Ed's benefit, not Teddy's. Teddy needs to learn that when he achieves, he is making progress toward his own goals, not his father's, and that this progress is its own reward. If you have a child like Teddy in your home, who has been programmed to look for treats and applause from you every time he (or she) accomplishes something, it will be useful to you to read the suggestions we later outline under "Motivation for the Long Term."

• **Impersonal learning.** Starting in middle school, teachers and school administrators (with some individual exceptions, of course) move increasingly to more impersonal means of instruction. Our society prefers a European model of abstract, objective learning, which reaches its peak in the undergraduate lecture hall where Dr. Expert lectures to a faceless mass of students who are focused on the knowledge being imparted (and who may never know Dr. Expert as a person—or become known by him). For some unknown percentage of students, however, this really doesn't work well. This latter group learns best when there is a close relationship between students and their teachers. These students want to see some interpersonal point to what they are learning—how the knowledge being imparted can actually help them or help them help other people. This preference is for *relational learning*.

It is likely that Teddy is such a relational learner, especially in view of his strong preference for social interaction. Different teaching techniques are needed for students who prefer relational learning. How to tell whether your child is a relational learner, and what to try if he is, are topics discussed in the "Relational Learning" section of this chapter.

• **Having intelligence the school system doesn't reward.** Educational researchers have identified seven types of intelligence, though most schools value only two of them. The other kinds of intelligence, though, can be quite valuable in adult life. Teddy seems to have a good bit of interpersonal intelligence, as shown by his above-average social skills and leadership qualities. While this form of intelligence may seem like giving in to a distraction now, Ed is unwise to condemn it categorically. Later in life, interpersonal intelligence may be the very skill that enables Teddy to become a successful salesperson or make a career in business. How to build on your child's natural individual strengths, while not ignoring the necessary requirements of school, will be discussed in the section "Fostering Multiple Intelligences."

Your child may have one or more of these issues, or, like Teddy, be coping with them all. Whatever the case, don't get discouraged. As the fable of the tortoise and the hare reminds us, the race is not always to the swiftest. Learning to understand your "unmotivated" child and exploring the options you have as a parent can help you help your child to a happy finish line.

## First Things First

There are physical conditions that can delay a child's progress or cause her to appear passive and uninterested. So it is an important first step to consult with your child's pediatrician. Describe the school difficulties your child is having, and ask that she be evaluated in particular for any developmental delays. Allergies and frequent ear infections, for example, can delay speech and language development in particular.

Your child should also have vision and hearing evaluations. The screenings typically performed at public schools are rudimentary; they can tell you if your child is very nearsighted or has a major hearing loss, but they will not pick up more subtle difficulties. It is worthwhile to arrange full evaluations with an optometrist or ophthalmologist and with an audiologist—your pediatrician can make referrals.

With the optometrist or ophthalmologist, ask that your child be checked for farsightedness as well as nearsightedness. Farsighted children, those who can see far away clearly but have trouble seeing what is up close, are almost never picked up in routine vision screenings. But this condition can cause eye strain and make a child avoid reading. Another condition to ask about is scotopic-sensitivity syndrome, when the eyes are sensitive to fluorescent light in particular, and words blur when the child tries to read. While it is comparatively rare, 25,000 people in the United States wear colored filters to aid their reading because of scotopic-sensitivity syndrome. Wearing filters, or reading words on colored paper, generally eliminates the problem. If your optometrist or ophthalmologist is not familiar with this condition, which was only recently discovered, contact the Irlen Institute to find someone near you trained in screening for scotopic-sensitivity syndrome.[2]

With the audiologist, ask about hearing conditions in which the child can hear normally in a one-to-one or small-group situation, but has trouble hearing when there is a lot of background noise (as in a crowded restaurant). Most elementary school classrooms are noisier than the average restaurant, and the child who repeatedly says, "But I didn't hear the teacher say that" may be telling the truth.

If everything checks out physically, ask your pediatrician for a general assessment of your child's developmental level. There is wide variability within the normal range. Would your pediatrician describe your child as a little behind, a little ahead, or just about the same as other children his age? Keep in mind this is an assessment of developmental level to date. Children develop at different rates, and a child who is behind her peers at the age of five may excel them all when she's twenty-five. Unless there is some actual condition causing developmental delay, such as Down's syndrome, a developmental lag is generally just a function of pace and a response to the life experiences the child has had.

If your child is slightly behind, though, make sure you are providing enough intellectual stimulation at home. Having a wide variety of interactive experiences is most stimulating for children intellectually. For example, you should provide experiences like cooking and going to the park and talking with you, as opposed to passive experiences, such as watching television, that don't require much of the child and don't involve interaction with adults.

## Developmental Readiness

In all cultures in which children learn to read and write, this education begins between the ages of five and seven. Somewhere within that age range, children become more educable, more able to reason, more understanding of cause and effect, and less physically restless. But there is wide individual variability. In particular, boys tend to lag behind girls in their readiness for formal education.

It would make more educational sense to wait for each child to be ready for his formal education to begin, instead of having an arbitrary age cutoff. But it would be administratively cumbersome to test each individual child. So both private and public schools tend to set up a birthday requirement, usually that the child must be six by September 1 to start first grade.

(Private schools are often more flexible about this requirement.) This means that in every first grade classroom, some children have just turned six, while others are already seven.

Over time the children who start off behind catch up, at least developmentally. But they may lose out both academically and socially because of their premature start. A boy who has just turned six, compared with a girl who is seven or close to it, is going to appear clumsier, more physically aggressive, less able to pay attention, and less verbal. The danger is not that he will not eventually catch up but that in the meantime he is going to start thinking of himself as stupid or awkward. He may also fail to understand some of the basic concepts he is supposed to be learning. And his teachers and classmates may form a negative impression of him, an impression that will be passed on to next year's teacher and become difficult to erase.

Before starting first grade, a child should be readily able to

- share and take turns;
- separate from her parent(s) for a few hours without great distress;
- communicate his needs clearly—for example, be able to ask a strange teacher for a bathroom break and where the toilet is located;
- hold a pencil and cut with scissors (these are important fine-motor skills);
- sit quietly by herself doing class work and sit in a small group during story time or a similar activity, without disrupting the process.[3]

The first-grade teachers in your child's school will be able to give you a more specific list, depending on what their goals and expectations are. In balance, however, especially with boys, if there is doubt, add that extra year of kindergarten. The only child to whom this would not apply is the accelerated child (see Chapter 4).

Starting first grade is a huge transition in a child's life, but it is not the last such transition. For many children, moving from elementary to middle school is just as big a transition. In middle school, children have to move from class to class, and teachers take a less parental role, expecting that children will be more able to fend for themselves. Middle schools are also typically far larger, and some children feel lost.

As with elementary school, it helps to wait until the child is ready, and it helps to practice first. The only way to delay the transition is to place your child in a smaller private school, where sixth grade is still a part of elementary school (or move to one of the few remaining school districts where this is the case). Practicing is usually easier to arrange. Talk to your child's elementary school guidance counselor early in his fifth-grade year about arranging for him to travel to another classroom for one or more subjects. Many elementary schools do this routinely, but if yours doesn't, it could still be arranged at your request and with coordination between the two teachers.

Another way to practice is to arrange a tour of the middle school your child will be attending, taking along your child, sometime in the spring semester of fifth grade. You can use this opportunity to make contact early with the sixth-grade guidance counselor, just in case there are problems in the fall. Ask parents whose children go to your child's elementary school if they have older children in middle school who would be willing to talk to your child, perhaps go out for a hamburger and a frank discussion over the summer. Before fifth grade ends, arrange with the parents of your child's closest friends to have a "reunion" at the end of the first week or so of middle school, or send home invitations, making sure you get phone numbers so you can follow up. Many of your child's elementary school friends may be in his classes in middle school, but some will not be. And for most children, it is immensely soothing to have such a reunion party, of all the girls who used to be in Mrs. X's fifth grade or everyone in the after-school chess club of Y elementary school, early on in middle school. It helps to make the point that all the children are in the transition together, and everyone will have first-day-of-middle-school stories to tell. You will find yourself quite popular with your child's friends for thinking of the reunion idea, and it will give your own child something pleasurable to anticipate.

## Repeating a Grade

 What if your child got off to a slow start? Or what if, in retrospect, you wish you had waited another year before first grade? Or that sixth grade was not already in middle school in your district? Is it effective to buy your child more time by holding her back a year in school?

This is a raging controversy in the educational field, and there simply is not one right answer.[4] Generally speaking, the debate is about how great the benefit is versus how much being held back costs the child. In other words, will any learning problems disappear as a result of the extra year? Will there be shame and social stigma? There is usually at least some small benefit because the child reviews familiar material, which will therefore be somewhat easier. There is unfortunately always a cost—peers can be merciless in their comments, and even well-meaning adults may assume there is something "wrong" with the child.

Both research and clinical anecdotes suggest that the age of the child makes a great difference. Being held back for an extra year of kindergarten can be very useful in terms of developmental catch-up, and it can be accomplished with a minimum of social cost. It is usually best to tell the child something simple, such as, "The school made a mistake about your birthday, and it turns out you are not quite ready yet."

Being held back to repeat first, second, or third grade is trickier. The social stigma is considerably higher, and it is more likely the problem is not simply developmental. Keep in mind that being held back will *not* help a child with an undiagnosed learning disability or with an emotional problem. It only helps the child catch up developmentally.

If a teacher wants to hold your child back in kindergarten, first, second, or third grade, we recommend that you get a copy of the Gesell Institute's book on age-appropriate development for your child's specific age.[5] Perhaps read through not only the volume for your child's particular age but also the ones for the years immediately below and above your child's age. Notice ways in which your child is "average," behind, or ahead of schedule for common developmental tasks. You can observe your child's playing or working in groups of other same-age children (a helpful, though not particularly precise, measure). In this way you can establish whether you agree that your child is developing a bit more slowly in most areas, and would therefore benefit from an extra year to catch up.

You should see developmental issues or readiness across the board as you consider repeating a grade. If your child is having trouble in school *and* needs more help at home with basic self-care tasks, tends to play with younger children, and is not able to throw a ball or run as well as other children her age, to cite some specific examples, then it may help to have extra time to become ready. On the other hand, if your child is at or above developmental level in all other areas *except* reading and those tasks that require reading, it is more likely that what you are dealing with is a learning disability—an issue only of reading. Difficulties in only one area require specialized help, not overall delay. (For recommendations regarding possible learning disabilities, see Chapter 5.)

Consider any reasons you can think of why your child might be somewhat delayed. Common reasons include a having a September birthday, having had frequent ear infections, moving from one district to another (particularly from a rural district to a more advanced urban area), the family's frequent moves, or the child's frequent absences from school. Considering these factors will help you calmly explain the decision to your child, should you decide to go with the teacher's recommendations and hold the youngster back a year. If you are uncomfortable with your child's being held back, this is your decision to make and you should be the final arbiter. However, do consider what the teacher is saying.

The impetus to hold a child back usually comes from the teacher's suggestion. However, if it does not come from the teacher—that is, if you are the one who would like your child held back and the teacher doesn't recommend it—please reconsider. Although it is still your decision, teachers deal with many more children of a given age group than do most parents, and if the teacher thinks your child is more or less typical, she probably is. If you have concerns, consider motivation as an issue instead.

We do not recommend holding children back in the older elementary grades unless there is an exceptional reason (e.g., lengthy absence due to illness) to do so. Holding children back in middle and high school significantly increases the chance they will drop out of school and exposes them to considerable social stigma; it is to be avoided if at all possible. Summer school and after-school tutoring are preferable alternatives.

## Motivation for the Long Term

You may have laughed at Teddy's poor father, manipulated into promising the boy an expensive toy just for keeping his grades up. But this is a very common trap, one that snares many well-meaning parents. The child starts out a little behind, perhaps due to development. Or, perhaps, the child gets average grades and is developmentally appropriate for his age group, but the parent has above-average expectations. Either way, the parent starts out offering a little extra "encouragement." Before the parent knows what happened, the extra encouragement has become expected, and the child is frankly escalating the bidding war.

The reason for this demanding behavior is not that the parent is unreasonable, or the child greedy (except insofar as all children are a bit greedy, given human nature). The reason for the problem is that the child has come to rely on external motivation rather than on the intrinsic joy of learning or the internal reward that comes from achieving a personal goal. This is not a desirable situation: while hard work is often rewarded in life, the rewards are seldom immediate. The medical school student studying all night may be rewarded with an M.D. degree and a comfortable income, but these come after many years down the road, and while the student is studying, she must rely on her own sense of accomplishment as she finishes each task. Children who look around for an external reward every time they do what they are supposed to be doing in school are not learning good patterns for later life.

So what can you do if you get caught in the reward trap? With stubborn situations, it may take a while to change the pattern. But, with patience, it can be done. We suggest the following steps:

## Scale Back

Talk with your child about your perception that the rewards are getting out of hand. Rather than scolding or blaming, it is more effective to tell the child he is more mature now and ready to learn about "the real world." Few children can resist that invitation—it is our adult world, and children are most curious about the world of "real life." Explain your new plan: you will reward for effort, teach by consequences, and foster internal motivation. But you will also get rid of distractions, brace for the worst, and deal with your own issues; you don't need to announce these steps, as they are adult business. Keep the focus on how the child is now ready to learn about adult life and the world of work.

## Reward for Effort

Praise your child verbally when you see her studying or doing homework. Talk with your child's teacher, and praise your child when you hear reports of industry and hard work. Ask your child's teacher to notice and praise these things as well. A grade of A, B, or even C in a difficult class (e.g., algebra the first time it is introduced) is worthy of praise if the child has studied hard, done extra makeup assignments, asked for extra help, and completed all homework. But a B in an easier class, say Health, which would have been an A if the child had bothered to turn in required worksheets, is not something you want to praise. Grades can be misleading; notice and praise *effort*. And keep the rewards intangible—a few positive words, a hug, or an extra privilege such as staying up a little later at night. In adult life, your boss doesn't buy you a present every time you have to work hard, and this is not something you want to lead your child to expect from life.

## Teach by Consequence

Set a reasonable baseline of expectations, and communicate this to your child. In elementary school, this usually means no grades below a B. In middle and high schools, you probably want to make provision for an occasional C in a difficult class, so change that to a B average or make the point that you will be factoring in effort. If the child doesn't perform up to this standard, your attitude should be that this is a problem, *not* because you are personally disappointed or hurt but because the child is not accomplishing what she needs to accomplish for her own goals in life. The *consequence* should be something that makes sense, such as having to retake the class in summer school or having to retake the class by correspondence. Or, if it is simply one bad grade rather than a failed class, the consequence might be spending a couple of weekday afternoons with a tutor or cutting back on extracurricular activities.

Be prepared to enforce this consequence, probably several times. This is the "bracing for the worst" we mentioned earlier. Your child has been used to being rewarded for every little thing, and he will probably test you to see if he can hook you back into the older reward system—perhaps by his failing a few tests, maybe even a class or two. Hang in there. Make sure you have talked with each of his teachers to let them know you are trying to establish an intrinsic reward system with consequences for not expending effort and that your child may rebel against it for a while. Most teachers will be very supportive and will stick firmly to their expectations of the child as well. Hold firm to your consequence, and otherwise don't dwell on the failure(s).

## Remove Distractions

We already mentioned cutting down on the child's extracurricular activities. Such extras as clubs and classes, vacations during the school year, television on school nights, and friends over during the week should be removed when your child is not working in school. Don't explain this as a punishment but as a help. ("You're having trouble getting your homework done, so I will help you have time to do it, by removing the television and video games during the week.") These treats can come back, in small doses, as rewards for effort. Remember to reward primarily effort, not results, since results can vary according to the subject and the teacher.

## Deal with Your Own Issues

Ed always wanted to go to an Ivy League college, but his folks didn't have the money. Parents often have these "leftover" issues from their own lives, but it doesn't help to involve children in them. The grades Teddy makes in elementary school won't affect his entrance into college one way or the other. (Grades start "counting" for college admission at the ninth-grade level. And they are only one of many factors that admissions officials consider.) Even if the grades did count now, in the unlikely event that Teddy was admitted to a very selective institution, given his low level of interest in school it would be a waste of time and money all around. Separate out your own issues from what will actually affect your child's life. If you find you can't distinguish your issues from his, talk this over with a qualified family therapist.

## Foster Internal Motivation

Sooner or later your child needs to get interested in accomplishing his own goals, not just in pleasing you or his teacher. Parents can do two extremely helpful things to foster their children's self-motivation. The first is to explore interests that tie in with school, something that is most helpful in the elementary and middle school years though it can continue into high school as well. You know what tends to interest your child. Find out what your child is studying in school, and set up activities that tie together your child's spontaneous interests with the school-related topics. For example, if your child is interested in art and is studying ancient Egypt at school, a trip to an art museum featuring Egyptian or Egyptian-inspired art is in order. If your child is studying fractions and likes football, watch a televised football game together and involve him in trying to figure out what percentage of a team's first downs are passing rather than running plays. Make it a point to do something at least once a week that builds on your child's interests.

The other, even more effective tool you have to spark your child's interest in school is introducing the world of work. This is easiest to do in high school, of course, but with a little creativity you can use the concept in middle and even elementary school. At every stage, make sure it is clear that rewards are tied to work—that there is no free lunch in life. Certainly by the time your child is in high school, he or she ought to have to earn money for such "extra" expenses as car insurance (if he wants his own car) or additional fashionable clothes (if she wants to outdress her friends).

A summer job is a great learning experience. If your child gets interested in the work, you have a jumping-off place from which to discuss careers. If, more likely, your child finds it boring to flip hamburgers, distasteful to clean up after customers, and unpleasant to deal with a demanding boss, you have the perfect opportunity to point out what kind of jobs you can get with a good education, and exactly what the alternatives are.

Even before the child is of legal working age, encourage her to pursue volunteer work in an area of interest and to work for you around the house. Again, your goal is to give your child a dose of the real world. So don't be an unreal employer. In adult life no one is going to pay you $20 for half-heartedly vacuuming the living-room carpet, and neither should you do that for your child. If you hire your child to work as a maid, gardener, or car washer, find out what the going rate is, pay only that, and don't pay at all if the job is not performed to your satisfaction. Any "job" should be distinct from, and over and above, the chores the child is required to do around the house, which should involve at a minimum picking up her own messes.

Volunteer work is another productive avenue to explore, and it can build a child's sense of accomplishment and start him thinking productively about future careers. If your child is interested in animals, see if you can arrange for him to volunteer at a vet's office or local animal shelter. If your child is interested in hanging out at the mall, see if she can work with a local merchant to stock inventory and learn about how retail business works. If you are a working parent without much time to spend with your child, volunteering together can be a particularly rewarding activity.

What you are building, by tying together your child's interests with her schoolwork and introducing her to the world of work, is internal motivation. What your child needs to develop is a sense of what interests her; how that might translate into a job, career, or lifelong interest; and, most of all, how good it feels to accomplish something difficult but worthwhile. These are much greater gifts than anything you could buy her.

## Relational Learning

Your child learns from you because he cares about you and knows he is important to you. That interpersonal dimension of learning is important to all children, but especially important to some children. Some children learn much better when they feel their instructor cares about them. In elementary school,

## From a Former Delayed Child

**H**ere is an actual story that well illustrates the reality of a school system's selling short a youngster. Stephen (not his real name) works for a large city as an urban planner in charge of zoning and development. He tells us of his earlier "backward" days in school.

"I was what they called 'backward.' Starting back in kindergarten, the teacher would set me in the corner most of the day. I was a little young when I started, and my parents were recent immigrants from Hungary. I didn't speak English any too well either, and I didn't always understand what the teacher wanted. All I knew was they never seemed to be happy with me, and everything I did, I got in trouble for it. This kid, Johnny, he stole my notebook, and so when I got it back, I whacked him over the head with it. That seemed fair to me, but I got in trouble for it, and they sent me to the corner again. Once we were supposed to memorize the 'Good Morning Song,' and I got some of it wrong. You guessed it—back to the corner. I didn't really mind—it was nice and peaceful there—but I minded about disappointing my dad.

"Every Saturday I would go to work with my dad and help him paint. He was a housepainter, with a whole crew of assistants. I was sort of like a junior assistant, but I helped with everything—mixing the paint, doing detail work, cleaning up, and even costing out the job pay. At work with my dad, I was somebody who was competent. I hung on to that all the years of sitting in the corner at school, thinking I was stupid. I used to sit there and figure out how many days it would take to complete a job, if we could afford to hire more help, that kind of thing. I was always good at figures.

"When I got into ninth grade, all of a sudden I had this straight-A report card. My parents were so proud. That is, they were proud until Mr. Kazinski came down from the apartment upstairs and told them I had been tracked into classes that wouldn't take me anywhere. I was taking all stuff like 'Print Shop,' 'Metalworking,' and 'Wood Shop.' I didn't know—I just went where they told me. But my dad went down and argued with the school. I will never forget that, and the faith he had in me. 'My son, he may not make such good grades all the time,' he said, 'but my son is going places. Take him out of these classes and put him back in with the other ones that are going places.' They did, and I went back to my C average, but I never forgot. Then, my senior year in high school, they had these advanced placement exams. I took European History, and there were questions about what led to World War II. Well, finally somebody was asking me an interesting question. All that time sitting in school, and mostly it was about things that didn't seem to have anything to do with me. But what led to the War, and how come my parents had to leave Hungary, I knew all about that. My dad and the other housepainters, they talked about nothing else. I made one of the highest scores in the state. When the results came in, I found out later, the school officials went through the roster three times, trying to see if there was not some other Stephen Laszlo. They couldn't believe it was me.

"On the strength of that exam score, I got into a fairly good college. There I continued to be up and down. If the course interested me, and there were a number that did such as history and finance and how to make livable communities, I did well. If it didn't, well, I didn't. Like Shakespeare—my wife tries to explain him to me, but frankly I got through that class entirely with Cliff Notes. Sometime in college I found what I wanted to do, and in graduate school I was like a man on fire. Zoning, budgets, figuring out how to get a community center built, dealing with the people who call city hall to complain—there's never a dull moment, and I have to admit I love all of it.

"I am one of the youngest ever to hold my position, and I do very well at it. Part time, I am getting my doctorate in public administration. On one of my doctoral papers, my instructor wrote, 'You have both a passion for social justice and a keen financial brain.' Well, yeah. I had that back in elementary school, too, but they sure as hell weren't interested. I'm just glad I had someone like my dad, who let me do real work and didn't treat me so much like a kid. My advice to parents is, be like he was."

these are the children who do best with a nurturing teacher. In middle school, the transition to a group of teachers may be painful, especially if the classes are large and the atmosphere impersonal. Such children can get lost by high school, and begin to tune out on education.

I teach in a graduate program in marriage and family therapy, and a certain percentage of the students in this program, too, seem to fall into this category. They were admitted with only average college records but with great references and volunteer experience, and they have turned into outstanding graduate students. The opportunity to focus on courses that relate to people and offer practical experience in the field brings out their best work. I suspect this is true of other helping professions as well.

If you notice your child responds best when his teacher takes a personal interest in him, or blossoms when her efforts directly involve other people, there are ways you can foster this type of interpersonal learning—to make sure your child makes it to that graduate-school haven. In elementary school let the guidance counselor know your child does best with a nurturing teacher, and work to build your own relationships with your child's teachers, so the personal network is reinforced. In middle school encourage your child to join an after-school club sponsored by one of her teachers. (It may help to let the middle school guidance counselor know that you would like for your child to be placed with at least one teacher who sponsors such a club.) Then do your best to foster a relationship with this particular teacher.

In middle and also high school, your child may benefit from a mentor, arranged by the school. If the school does not have a mentoring program, find out if your child could tutor a younger child who is having trouble in school. The most recent Department of Education–sponsored study on peer tutoring found that children who are somewhat behind academically actually improve *more* from tutoring another child than from being tutored themselves. I suspect this is because they thrive on the interpersonal closeness they can get from teaching— and the sense of accomplishment.

Volunteer work is another wonderful way to make sure your child gets that connection with others. Volunteer experience is also very attractive to college admissions counselors, and helps compensate for indifferent grades or other difficulties. For maximum benefit, choose work that involves close relationships with others (handing out food to the homeless, say, rather than stacking donated canned goods) and that ties in with possible future careers. An example of a career link might be working with young children at a day-care center, with staff members who are licensed teachers and potential mentors, rather than simply babysitting in the neighborhood.

## Fostering Multiple Intelligences

Relational learners like to work closely with people, and the ability to work well with others can be seen as a skill or a talent. Logically, it seems likely to be at least as useful a talent as the ability to do math problems in one's head or to read a complicated text quickly. But it is much less likely to be rewarded in school.

In 1983, Howard Gardner of Harvard University first proposed his concept of multiple intelligences.[6] Gardner contends that human beings actually are intelligent in seven different ways:

- Verbal (reading and writing)
- Logical-mathematical (numbers and logic)
- Visual-spatial (artistic, engineering, and spatial reasoning skills)
- Bodily-kinesthetic (learning by doing, crafts and athletic skills)
- Musical (listening, performing, and composing kinds of musical talent)
- Interpersonal (influencing others, "people smarts")
- Intrapersonal (empathizing with others, knowledge about oneself)

For an entertaining introduction to this theory, and to explore your own preferences, log onto the interactive multiple intelligence site at www.surfaquarium.com/im.htm.[7] You will be invited to select and try out a variety of games. Most likely, some of these games will appeal to you far more than others. I was most eager to try the Temperament Sorter (utilizes intrapersonal intelligence), but my eleven-year-old daughter went straight to the BrainTeaser puzzles (mathematical-logical intelligence), and my husband was intrigued by the Build It and Bust It game (bodily-kinesthetic intelligence). This website, run by an educational consultant, is not designed for you to scientifically assess your type of intelligence. As Gardner points out, all humans have and can use all seven types of intelligence. But most of us have a preference for one or two, and trying out these games is a fun way to notice your preferences and to recognize that everyone does not have the same preferences.

Despite educational theory, schools still typically reward only two of these seven types of intelligence: verbal and logical-mathematical. One can be a genius at influencing others, a musical prodigy, or a star athlete, and still have a hard time in school. These talents will be quite useful in later life, however.

If your child's interests are not academic—if her strengths lie in one or more of the five intelligences *not* directly rewarded in school—it is still important to build upon these natural interests, where her talents may lie. Avoid negative talk about the child's alternative strengths ("If you spent as much time studying as you do drawing those stupid pictures, you could maybe bring your grades up!" "What good is athletics going to do you?"). Instead, look for ways that the child's strengths and interests tie in with assigned schoolwork. Magnet schools in the area of interest are perfect for this type of child. Volunteer work and internship opportunities are also useful. Certainly your child still has to do the reading, writing, and arithmetic. But rather than criticizing his or her other abilities, build on them, tie them in with the required work, and keep an eye on the future, when all types of talents will be useful.

## Family Activity

To explore motivation and learning styles in a fun way, log on to www.lightspan.com. This is a commercial site, but it offers free "snapshots" (mini-assessments) of motivational and learning-style patterns. Click on "Parents," then on "Tools and resources," and then on "Snapshot assessments." Don't take this too seriously—it does not substitute for a formal assessment—but it is a great conversation starter.

# School Choices for the Delayed Child

Slower development, motivational issues, and a child's having "different" interests may all play a role in a youngster's lagging behind in school. As a parent, you and your child can avail yourselves of the options we have just discussed, but you may also consider alternative school choices. Smaller classes and smaller schools are generally preferable for a child who isn't strongly motivated or one who may get lost in a large, impersonal environment. I most often recommend a private school, when this is an option, for these kinds of children. A small religious school or a preparatory school in which teachers are willing to work with a youngster who shows a little underachieving in the beginning may be a good choice. There your child can get the individual attention he or she needs.

If this change of school is not an option, it can work just as well to work closely with your child's teachers, to prevent her from getting lost in the crowd, and to add extra stimulation at home. I generally do not recommend home schooling for this type of child, as it is too easy for a parent to get caught up in pushing, rewarding, and threatening. In that situation the learning process becomes more the parent's than the child's. The detached, neutral strategies of rewarding effort and teaching by consequence are hard enough to hold on to when there are outside teachers available to provide some of the structure. But there are always exceptions, and if the public school system available to you is so impersonal as to overwhelm your child, and you are confident of your ability to take just enough responsibility and no more, home schooling remains an option.

Finally, consider encouraging your child to make the move early from school to work. Some of the most burned-out teenagers I have seen are those whose interests and talents are *not* primarily academic (verbal and mathematical-logical, in Gardner's terms), who work steadily at school, but see little reward beyond average grades and a future of more of the same. For such a youngster, an interesting summer job can be a real motivator. So can part-time vocational programs within the public schools, usually starting in tenth grade, which allow the student to work part-time in the afternoon and take courses in the morning. The courses remain fully college preparatory, and most of these programs require that the student keep his grades up, a good incentive.

In extreme cases, consider moving the child to vocational school. I once worked with a fourteen-year-old girl who had lost all interest in school. Owing to a variety of family problems (more about those in Chapter 7), she had managed to miss most of her ninth-grade year. She had little interest in returning to her traditional school. In fact, she seemed to have few interests in life other than her long, carefully manicured fingernails. When I commented on her careful grooming, she perked up for the first time and told me she did manicures for several of her friends as well. Building on this hint of an interest, her parents ultimately enrolled her in a local vocational school, where she could study cosmetology. Like other vocational schools that accept students who have not yet graduated from high school, the school provided for her to obtain her GED (general equivalency degree) at the same time as the cosmetology certification.[8] With this, she was able to begin a career. Further, with her interests sparked, she ultimately enrolled in college to obtain a degree in fashion design. Most important, she regained her enthusiasm and could formulate positive plans for the future.

## What Not to Do

Whether because of the individual's nonacademic interests, particular pace and timing, or motivations not yet fully awakened, a child who tends to underachieve can be frustrating to parents and teachers. But it is important not to let the school solve this frustration problem for you by tracking your child into remedial classes. While these classes are easier for a student to pass, many of them are not college preparatory. Therefore, they cut off options for your child prematurely, without providing a vocational fallback.

This can happen without your even being aware of it, as remedial classes are no longer called *remedial*. In an effort to spare students' feelings (and allay parental concerns), these classes have generally been renamed. For example, at my stepdaughters' suburban high school, students are tracked into one of the following, in ascending order of difficulty: "regular," "advanced," "honors," "advanced placement," or "gifted" classes. The "regular" classes are in fact remedial, and students taking these classes are not expected to go on to college.

Don't let the system sell your child short in this way. Requesting that your child be moved to a higher level class, switching to a small private school, and switching to a vocational school would all be options offering your child more of a future.

## TEACHER TIPS

Here are some strategies from our teacher consultant to show you how to aid your child's teacher in helping your child catch up and regain enthusiasm for school.

### Tell Me About Your Child's Motivation

I'm not a mind reader, and it's not likely your child will volunteer to me that he finds me dull or is only turning in homework to please you. I don't get as much chance as you to see what interests and motivates your child. Let me know, for example, that your child loves to be a leader socially, and maybe I can put him in charge of a small-group activity. Let me know she loves to play basketball, and I can make up some math word problems about basket heights. Stephen had some negative experiences, but most teachers today will work with you, if you give them enough information to be useful allies.

### Ask About Alternative Projects

I need to evaluate your child's progress, as I do the progress of every child I teach. Sometimes that has to be in a particular format, such as a nationally standardized exam or an essay (when the purpose is to teach how to write essays). But sometimes the format can vary. When your child is asked to write a book report, for example, it may be that a teacher would be open to his turning in a painting of the book's climactic scene, or setting the story to music, or building a 3-D diorama instead of writing a standard report. Science and social studies fairs offer a particular opportunity for such creative projects. In this way your child can have a chance to shine, doing what he does best, even if it's not part of the standard curriculum.

### Tell Me About the Whole Child

I want to teach your child as a whole person, but it may be that I only get to see a narrow slice of his behavior during school hours. Drop by to see me, and let me know that your child just won an award, is the most trusted babysitter in your neighborhood, or trained the dog to do six new tricks—whatever you think I need to know to fully appreciate your child. By the same token, remember that I am not a cardboard figure who has no feelings and no life outside the classroom; talk about me to your child as a whole person, with respect.

### Set Structure and Limits

If a child has some struggles with school, then her completing homework, attending school regularly, and being on time for school become especially important tasks. I count on you to provide that structure, so that your child doesn't start off the day behind already.

### Let's Talk Often

There are lots of questions that your child's teacher can't answer without consulting you: for example, whether a child should repeat a grade in school, what is causing an apparent lack of motivation, whether a child has important interests outside of school. And I hope you won't try to answer these kinds of questions without consulting with your child's teacher. Teamwork does help!

# Resources

These are some print resources that can help you further explore the topics discussed in Chapter 3:

For more information on multiple intelligences, see Howard Gardner, *Intelligence Reframed: Multiple Intelligences for the 21st Century* (New York: Basic Books, 2000).

For more information about the concept of relational learning and how it relates to gender and cultural diversity, read J. Anderson and M. Adams, "Acknowledging the Learning Styles of Diverse Student Populations," *New Directions for Teaching and Learning* 49 (1992): 19–32.

# 4

# "I'm Bored!"

## *The Accelerated Child*

Becky is five years old. Her kindergarten class is learning about winter. The teacher passes out a worksheet with a printed illustration of a winter scene, and directs the children to color the snowflakes. All the other children get out their crayons and begin to color, but Becky's hand is already waving in the air. "Snowflakes are white and the paper is white," she reports, "so there is not any point in us coloring." The teacher sighs. Becky is always so difficult.

Josh is nine. His fourth-grade class has just completed a science unit on plants, and now the students are taking an exam. Josh answers each question correctly, moving quickly through the multiple-choice portion of the exam. Then he comes to the one essay question. The question is "What three things have you learned from this unit?" Josh prints neatly, "I did not learn anything, because I already knew it." The teacher marks this answer wrong, impatient with what she views as Josh's disrespect. As the essay question is worth 50 percent of the exam, Josh's grade is correspondingly low, surprising his biologist mother who wonders why her bright child doesn't do better in school.

Laura is fifteen. Her teachers think she is a high-average student, earning mostly B grades. What they do not know is that Laura earns these B's despite never opening a textbook or putting in any time to study. In class she mostly daydreams. Of late, her daydreams have focused on a law student she met at the coffee shop where she likes to hang out. Laura is fascinated to hear about the books he is reading and what his life is like in graduate school. She has always felt older than the other girls her age, and has difficulty sharing their interests, so it feels natural to her to gravitate to friends a decade older than she is. Her parents have no idea she is thinking about dropping out of school next year and taking a job at the coffee shop to help her newfound beau with his student loans. After all, Laura reasons, school has always been boring for her—a definite waste of time.

Becky, Josh, and Laura are all of above-average intelligence. Why, then, are they not doing well in school? They are at risk for three reasons:

1. **School systems are primarily designed to serve the child functioning within a normal range of intelligence.** The classroom teacher must address her- or himself to the majority of the children in the classroom. This means that children who are significantly ahead of the rest of the class might have trouble getting their needs met, just as might children who are significantly behind. Decades of educational research have shown that without special intervention children who are ahead of schedule developmentally are significantly more likely than average children to develop discipline problems early in their

school years. And they are more likely to drop out before finishing high school.[1] This is why concerned parents have lobbied
for special programs for "gifted and talented" youngsters. Legislation before both the House and the Senate (The Gifted and
Talented Students Education Act of 1999) would increase federal funding of these special programs and bring some consis-
tency nationwide to the criteria used by individual states for
determining inclusion.

**2. Intelligent children tend to challenge authorities.** Young
children who are unusually verbal and curious tend to ask more
questions and challenge more premises. This simply reflects
their developing intellect, rather than any malice toward authority. But adults often become impatient with a child who always
seems to be questioning them. Factual statements from the
child, such as Josh's comment that he had already learned the
material at home, may be met with skepticism or viewed as
"showing off." Over time, perceiving that teachers and other
adults get annoyed when they speak out too often, verbally
gifted children may silence themselves. They are then at risk for
becoming like Laura, physically but not mentally present in the
classroom.

**3. Academic intelligence is not common sense.** Becky is
way ahead of the other children in her kindergarten class when
it comes to reading readiness, but she doesn't understand that
she is annoying her teacher. Josh will probably make a fine sci-
entist one day, but right now he needs to learn a little more tact.
And Laura considers herself older than she actually is, mistak-
ing her genuinely advanced intellectual abilities for maturity
and experience of the world.

Becky, Josh, and Laura would all score significantly above
the norm on a standardized intelligence test. Such children are
described by most school systems as "gifted." Gifted, however,

is a somewhat confusing and emotionally loaded word. It might be argued that all children are "gifted," and certainly each child has unique gifts. But if your child's gifts are musical or mechanical, for example, he or she won't necessarily be insufficiently challenged by grade-level reading and mathematics. The term *gifted* is meant to describe a child who learns academic material quickly, and so gets ahead of the regular schedule for learning in the classroom.

In this chapter we will refer to such children as "accelerated." Keep in mind, however, that your local school system probably instead uses the terms *gifted*, *gifted and talented*, or *high aptitude*. If your child shows talent in a nonacademic area (such as athletics, automobile repair, or drawing), you might want to review the discussion in Chapter 3 on multiple kinds of intelligence.

## First Step: Gather Evidence

If you suspect that your child may be accelerated academically, you can take the steps to develop a picture of what may be happening. At this stage, don't let the school know you suspect giftedness. It is too easy to discount such a theory as parental pride; you'll need to gather your evidence first.

### Talk with Your Child

As always, your child is your first and best source of information. Children who are academically ahead of schedule, and consequently bored in school, tend to describe themselves as bored or frustrated, saying that school drives them crazy. They are unlikely to consistently describe themselves as being exhausted or as struggling or to complain that the work is too hard. They may complain that they are asked to do the same thing, over and over. They will typically complain loudest and longest about tasks that involve considerable repetition (coloring and simple worksheets in the primary grades; writing sentences assigned by the teacher in the later elementary grades; multiple choice exams in secondary school). Their favorite school days involve some break in the routine: a field trip, guest speaker, or special class project. The teacher may comment that on such special days, the child's behavior is not a problem. (Contrast this with the delayed child, described in Chapter 3, and the inattentive child, described in Chapter 6, both of whom will often be the most difficult for the teacher on such days).

## Observe Your Child at School, Home, and Play

Contrary to the stereotype of the bright child who is scorned by his peers yet a "teacher's pet," most accelerated children are leaders of their peer groups. Their age mates come to them because these leaders are good at inventing games and seldom run out of ideas for things to do. Their friends will often describe them as "bright," "funny," and "interesting." They may also be described as "bossy," however, especially in the elementary years. They can become impatient with peers who can't or won't follow their complicated directions for play. For example, one accelerated nine-year-old grew frustrated with the other girls at her birthday party when they wanted to watch a video, rather than play autopsy with a replica model of the human heart. Perhaps surprisingly, however, the eccentricities of such children are tolerated well for the most part; other children apparently consider that putting up with a little bossiness is a fair trade for the interesting ideas (and, occasionally, trouble) that this accelerated child can generate.

Often, the accelerated child may gravitate toward older children, and even adults, who are better able to share his or her interests. This can place the accelerated teenager at risk for unsuitable romantic relationships. A bright teenage boy, for example, may be drawn to what he perceives as the intellectual conversation and adult interests of a woman in her thirties, and not possess sufficient knowledge of the world to wonder why she is spending time with a teenage boy instead of a man. Plenty of academic challenge in school, which keeps the child well occupied, and the company of other accelerated children and young adults are the best protections against such age-inappropriate relationships. It is worth remembering, however, that a child may be academically far ahead of schedule and still be very much in need of adult protection. The quick learning curve of the accelerated child does not guarantee common sense or practical knowledge, just a zest for academics.

Adults often find an accelerated child delightful to talk with, almost like a peer. Such children are challenging, however, and quick to question rules, especially if they don't immediately understand the reason behind them. It takes a special kind of teacher to cope with the quick wit and challenges of this type of child, and this is why teaching the gifted has become a branch of special education, requiring additional training and special certification.

## Talk with Your Child's Teacher

It is unrealistic to expect your child's teacher to identify his or her academic giftedness. In repeated studies, researchers have found that teachers have been no more accurate than random chance in identifying those children in their classrooms who will score in the intellectually gifted range on a standardized intelligence test. Parents, however, tend to be quite accurate at predicting their child's score. This is because parents know their children more deeply and intimately than can even the best teacher. Most classroom teachers are trained to identify those children who are having difficulty mastering the material; they will not always be able to notice, especially in a crowded classroom, those children who are mastering it too easily.

However, your child's teacher can give you valuable information, which should also be considered. The teacher can tell you if your child is scoring at or above grade level on exams. (Homework and routine class work may be done carelessly or not at all, but even a bored accelerated child tends to rally for an exam.) Teacher complaints about challenging or disrespectful, "smart aleck" behavior may also be a clue.

## Examine Your Child's Homework

The written record of class homework or assignments can often be telling. A child who consistently misses the easier, simple problems at the beginning of an assignment—and then gets right the more difficult, complicated problems at the end of the assignment—may be a bored accelerated child. (Contrast this with the delayed child, described in Chapter 3, and the confused or overwhelmed child, described in Chapter 5, both of whom may start off doing well, then flounder as the assignment becomes more difficult and time-consuming.) The accelerated child may also change the assignment to make it more interesting. For example, one kindergartner, asked to count the four buttons on a gingerbread man's shirt, wrote out "five, though you only see four, because somebody already ate one." That child was finding counting too easy, and converted the question into a simple subtraction problem instead to pique her own interest and make a story of it. Similarly, an accelerated high school student, asked to turn in a simple factual report on the French Revolution, produced instead a long and thoughtful essay on the differences and similarities between the French and

American Revolutions. Again, it takes a flexible and often specially trained teacher to cope gracefully with this sort of surprise twist; in the regular classroom, such "improved" assignments may just get counted wrong.

If your child appears to you to be accelerated academically, then here are the next steps to take.

## Have Your Child's Intelligence Tested

Up until this point you have been keeping your suspicions quiet as you explored the possibility that your child is accelerated. But now it's time to raise the topic of giftedness with your child's school, and a score on a standardized intelligence test is the best way to open such a conversation. Generally, the Wechsler Child Intelligence Test is preferred, but check with your local school district's office of psychological services to get their recommendation on an appropriate test measure. In most states, children who score significantly above the norm on such a test are eligible for special-education services within the public schools. The specific score that the school will agree to consider "significantly above the norm" varies from district to district, often depending on such political considerations as how crowded the gifted programs already are. Pending federal legislation would regularize this. In the meantime, use these generally accepted test score categories as a guide:

- With an intelligence test score of 100 to 114, the person is considered upper normal
- With an intelligence test score of 115 to 129, the person is considered bright
- With an intelligence test score of 130 to 144, the person is considered gifted

## From a Former Accelerated Child

**M**y brother, Reed Hearon, is my interview subject for this category. Reed went through the public schools before education for the "gifted" was a special program. He is now a nationally acclaimed chef, named Chef of the Year in 1996 by *San Francisco Focus* magazine, and recipient of the James Beard Award for Best New Restaurant in the United States in 1997. He is an honors graduate from the University of Chicago an d the University of Texas in philosophy and mathematics. He left high school following his junior year, after several years of increasing boredom and frustration, and was accepted at the University of Chicago even without a high school degree, owing to his high test scores.

"What I chiefly remember about school is being bored all the time. There was too much that was repetitive and mechanical. When I went to Chicago, that was the first time I was really stimulated. I think that the big piece of advice that I can give is for people to reexamine how they look at school and work. The crime of the Industrial Revolution was that it led people to think that you worked for money, so that you would have the money to use in your leisure time. Instead, learning should be a joy, not a means to an end. Do what you love to do and then figure out how to make money at it. Surround yourself with people who are passionate and who care like you do.[2]

- With an intelligence test score of 145 to 159, the person is considered highly gifted
- And someone with an intelligence test score of 160 or above is considered profoundly gifted.

Psychologists freely concede that the existing tests are only accurate within a range of plus or minus three points, so it is unfair for a district to provide services for a child who scores 130 and not for a child who scores 129. Still, this does happen, and, going into the testing, it may be useful for you to know your district's arbitrary cutoff score. Naturally, this is not information you would want to share with your child.

Both intelligence and achievement testing are available without cost to the parent through the public schools. Particularly if your child's teacher agrees such testing would be useful, you may find this the most convenient option. Do not be misled, however, if you are told, "We can't test until we get a referral from the teacher," or "We'll have to study the child first and see if testing is warranted." Most schools have a team of professionals, including the guidance counselor and the special-education coordinator, who make up the "child study team" or the "child review team." This team will want to observe your child and offer its own impressions as well. But, regardless of its conclusions, you can insist on testing, and the school will be legally required to provide it. (See the Introduction for a more complete discussion of parents' rights.)

However, practically speaking, the school can relegate your request to the bottom of the waiting list if no one within the school agrees with you about the need for testing. After all, accelerated children generally perform at or above grade level, at least on exams, and are seldom physically violent, so the school psychologist with many children to assess may reasonably prioritize more urgent situations (in which children are failing school or are on the verge of expulsion). This kind of prioritizing is even more likely to occur when, as in my district, one psychologist is assigned to several different schools and must commute between them. If you are hearing that there will be a delay of six months or more before your child can be tested, consider getting your child tested privately.

Private testing should be done by a licensed clinical psychologist, with experience in academic-cognitive testing. It is wise to check with both the private psychologist and the school district's office of psychological services to see if the psychologist you are considering has worked with the school district before and is well respected by them. The district staff will be happy to give you this information, as they, like you, do not want a conflict later on arising from a poor working relationship between private psychologist and school.

You will want to have an introductory meeting with any psychologist you are considering. In this meeting, which you should attend without your child, you can explain what you have observed so far and ask that your child be evaluated for the local school district's "gifted" program. (If your district does not have a program, or if its criteria are not clear, just ask for an overall intelligence-test score.) Being specific about your goals for the testing is important, as the psychologist may otherwise assume that you also want tests administered to evaluate how your child is doing emotionally. Tests that measure emotional functioning are different from intelligence tests, and while more information may seem desirable, keep in mind that the more tests that are administered, the more expensive the evaluation. Private intelligence testing is already quite expensive, costing from $400 to $600 in most areas, so this can be a concern.

If you would like to go the private route but cannot afford the fee, you do have options. First, talk to several psychologists in your area about payment plans and other special arrangements. Since the advent of managed care, private practices are more difficult to maintain, and practitioners are becoming more flexible about payment schedules. Check with your insurance company as well, although most insurance companies do not cover intelligence testing. Medicaid and CHAMPUS (the armed services' insurance plan) do, however, cover it. In addition, if there is a nearby university with a graduate department of clinical psychology, talk with the chair of that department about having your child tested by a graduate student, who would be working under the supervision of a faculty person to gain experience. The cost may be considerably lower than with professionals, the graduate student's inexperience is offset by the supervisor's experience and knowledge, and the graduate student is likely to have great enthusiasm for the opportunity. Finally, many community agencies for mental health charge on a sliding scale basis for the psychological services they offer. If you approach an agency, be specific about your wish for intelligence testing, as counseling is less expensive for the agency to provide than is psychological testing, and will usually be offered to you first. Your local United Way can give you a list of mental health agencies in your community.

## Prepare Your Child for Testing and Its Consequences

Intelligence testing is an activity that requires cooperation; if your child does not cooperate (for example, refusing to answer questions or making up silly answers), the results will be worthless. Fortunately, this is one time that your child's precocious thinking can work for you. Pick a quiet, unstressful time to talk with your child about your concern that he or she may be bored in school. This is *not* the time to add your concerns, if any, about your child's behavior, or to explain the importance of education. What you want to convey is that in this matter you are willing to act as your child's ally, as indeed you are by setting up this testing. Tell the child when and where the test is scheduled. If you are going through your local public school to get this testing, make sure the school administrator has agreed to let you know this information well in advance (as she is required to do if you ask) of the test date. It is wise not to promise that the test will result in a changed or improved school program—or even to mention that possibility—as that has yet to be negotiated, and you do not want your child to feel like a failure for missing an arbitrary score cutoff. It often works well to explain that, whatever the results, the test will help you as a parent understand the situation better, and so become a more effective advocate for your child.

Appealed to as an ally, most accelerated children are flattered, pleased by their parent's wish for school to be a better experience for them, and intrigued by the idea of the testing experience as something new and different. With younger children in particular, it is useful to add that your child can best help you learn from the test results by answering every question he or she can, even the questions that seem "too easy." Explain that the psychologist already knows the answers to all the questions but is curious to see how well the child can do. This mild challenge is stimulating to an accelerated child. And it may avoid the dismay of one parent, with whom I worked, whose child told her after the testing, "That psychologist must not know very much. I told him he had to find out some of those answers on his own, and not to be asking me all the time."

You know your child best, so use that knowledge to create the right level of curious anticipation, without tipping the balance over and creating undue anxiety. Schedule the test for the time of day your child tends to perform best (that is, no 7 A.M. tests for a night owl), and make sure the child is healthy, well rested, and well fed. If your child wakes up sick or cranky on the day of the test, it *is* worth rescheduling the testing. Intelligence tests can be given only once a year, as otherwise the score is not valid, so there is only one opportunity a year to let the psychologist see your child at his or her best. Remember to stay calm yourself—the test results are only one piece of data among many, one piece of the jigsaw puzzle you are constructing as you help to show school personnel what you know of your child.

## Assemble Your Case

Once you get the test results, ask yourself if you want to go further down this path. If the results indicate some other kind of academic issue at work, perhaps a learning disability or something else unexpected, you may want to reconsider. The test may show no difficulty, but also that your child just doesn't score quite high enough to make the school district's cutoff for the gifted program. That does not necessarily mean you need to give up. If your child's score is close to the cutoff point, you may be able to argue that other factors should also be considered. It is widely thought that the available standardized intelligence tests contain some degree of unintended bias against ethnic minorities whose first language was not the language in which they were tested. It may also be biased against younger children whose abilities are primarily nonverbal (who may have mathematical abilities they can't yet express). If your child fits into one or more of these categories, it is worthwhile arguing that other factors should be considered besides the testing.

Extra enrichment in the regular classroom is still a possibility. In the situation that your child's test score was near the cutoff point and you thought there could have been bias in the testing measure, you might also want to consider repeating the testing the following year, while going ahead with what enrichment you can arrange for the present.

# Explore Your Options

To begin your conversation with the school's administrator and other personnel, explain that you would like to discuss the results of the test along with other information you have gathered (your observations and samples of your child's schoolwork). For this meeting you will want your child's teacher, the coordinator for exceptional-student education, and the guidance counselor to be present (at a minimum—other school personnel may choose to be involved as well). Present your impressions, and explain your belief that your child needs extra academic challenge to stay alert and motivated in school.

The first option to consider is extra enrichment in the regular classroom. This route is likely to be promoted by school staff members if there are no special classes already in place or if your child is not at this time meeting the district's test-score cutoff for its "gifted" program. This kind of enrichment involves enlisting the regular teacher(s) to provide extra challenges for your child. This may be as simple as giving him a different reading book—or as complex as allowing her to tutor other children in advanced math. When discussing ideas for this option, ask yourself these questions:

- **Does this sound realistic?** Observing your child's class, you should notice the size of the class and usual level of activity. Be wary of special activities that sound as if they would take an unrealistic amount of the teacher's time, as these activities may not happen on a regular basis. With the best intentions in the world, there is only so much a single classroom teacher can do.

- **Is this something my child could get excited about?** The enrichment activity won't work unless it is genuinely challenging for the child. For example, a third-grade child reading at the seventh-grade level will not be challenged by being allowed to use the fourth-grade reading book. You are the one who has the most complete picture of your child, so it is up to you to remind school personnel of the level of challenge needed.

• **Does the teacher sound enthusiastic about trying this?** If not, continue talking some more about why you see a need for this, keeping your tone respectful and polite and giving specific ideas to be tried. If the teacher's time is the problem, perhaps you or someone in your family could come into the classroom a few hours a week to supplement your child's experience. Consider also on-line resources and supplemental curriculums (addresses for these are listed under "Resources" at the end of this chapter).

The second, more comprehensive, option is a special-education class for the "gifted." At the elementary school level, this type of class typically is called a "pull-out" program. Your child stays with his or her regular classroom for morning announcements, recess, lunch, and so on—all the nonacademic activities of the day. For one to three hours a day, however, your child is called out to a special class, with a different teacher trained in "gifted" education. This means that you and your child both must be comfortable with your child's being called out of the regular classroom daily or every other day, for what all the other children will know is a "special" class. (Usually it is euphemistically called an *enrichment activity* or referred to by an acronym such as GATE [Gifted and Talented Education], but the other children will quickly figure it out.) There may be—will likely be—some mainly good-natured teasing about this. Still, the extra stimulation and contact with other accelerated children are well worth the teasing for most children who qualify for such a class. At the middle and high school levels your child is more likely to be placed in entirely separate classes. Gifted children are "tracked" into a whole schedule of higher-level classes within each grade; they rotate from class to class with peers at a similar academic level. Here any teasing becomes an issue primarily at lunchtime and after school, and the child may feel more protected by constantly being with his or her "special" group. If the level of these classes is appropriate and provides sufficient challenge, this can be a fine option.

While it is less likely, it is still possible you may be offered a third option. Instead of either a special class or extra enrichment in the regular classroom, the school may suggest that your child skip an entire grade, or move up midyear to a higher grade. This option is offered less often these days, because experience has taught educators in most school districts it is problematic. The academically accelerated child is not ahead of schedule in any other way. Moving the child up a grade puts the child together with older peers, and this often exposes the youngster to a lot that he isn't ready for. While it may not seem a big deal to have your eight-year-old daughter playing with nine-year-olds, consider whether you really want her to be going to middle or high school a year ahead of her age mates. Being physically less developed, shorter, less strong, and otherwise immature in appearance compared with classmates can be difficult for a young teenager. Being accelerated academically won't help a girl when she is the last in her class to need a bra, and it won't please a boy when he is two feet shorter than any other boy in the class. Nor will it prevent your child from being exposed to classmates experimenting with sex or drugs, a year or more before you and your child would otherwise have discussed these temptations.

In addition, skipping a grade often does not even overcome the problem it is meant to solve. Accelerated children may be years ahead of their age mates academically; if your child is doing college-level math, moving up a grade in elementary school won't make him any less bored. Accelerated children, like all children, can be uneven in their abilities, and may be unable to do some of the work at the next grade level while still bored by the other material offered in their best subjects. The educational trend over the last two decades, for these reasons, has been to keep accelerated children together with their own age group *and* to offer them special instruction in their areas of particular strength.[3]

The situation of high school students may be different, since for these older youths "skipping" may mean placing out of some classes and graduating early from high school. The academic atmosphere of college usually is more congenial to the accelerated young adult, who becomes free to pursue special interests and seek out challenging instructors. However, even in this case, consider whether your child is emotionally mature enough to make the transition to college, however academically ready. A year of community college, while living at home, is sometimes a good compromise, and many school districts will give high school credit for community college work. To find out about this, check directly with an admissions counselor at the community college, as this option is often not publicized by the school district.

As you negotiate and plan, share with your child that you are trying to work out the best possible educational placement. Older children (middle school and up) may wish to participate in meetings with the school administrators and staff and to comment on the options themselves. This is fine, even educational in itself, as long as you can be confident the child will not witness a tense battle between you and the school professionals. Keep the discussion friendly and polite; in that atmosphere, involving an older child may be quite useful. Younger children, however, have a hard time with so many options, most of which will never happen. For children of elementary school age it is best to explain to them the decision the adults have made, once all sides agree. This can be done at a later meeting with student, parent, and teacher.

If you are not pleased with the options presented to you by the public schools, private school is still another option you may consider. Some parents of accelerated children feel they have failed their intellectually talented child if they cannot afford a private school education. They haven't. Private schools generally offer firmer discipline, more structure, and smaller classes. While these are important considerations for some children, as discussed in other chapters, they are not critical for the accelerated child. The accelerated child is typically able to focus even in a crowd; kept busy, he or she won't create a major discipline problem. It's academic challenge that the accelerated child needs. Special programs within the public schools should allow your child to approximate the level of challenge presented by an academically rigorous private school.

Public schools may even have an advantage, in that they can easily separate out and "track" accelerated children, while private school administrators may be reluctant to offend any tuition-paying parents by making distinctions among the students. "All our students are gifted" is a frequent quote one hears from private school headmasters. If you hear this, ask questions to make sure the special needs of your child will be met. All children have unique gifts, but not all children are academically accelerated, and this reality should not be glossed over. You should seek a private-school alternative for your accelerated child only when the youngster is unable for some reason to qualify for a "gifted" program within the public schools, you are unable to convince your child's regular teacher to add sufficient extra challenge, and you feel your child is growing increasingly bored and restless. In that situation, home school-ing and nationwide "talent search" programs are options to consider along with private schools.

It is likely, since you were a part of your child's becoming accelerated to begin with, that you already plan a good many enriching educational activities in your home. In addition, accel-erated children typically learn well with minimal guidance; they are relatively self-motivated. So home schooling can be a viable and inexpensive alternative for accelerated children. It will be challenging, however, to keep up with your accelerated child's constant need for the stimulation of new materials (new books, new computer software, more advanced activities) in a home setting.

The home schooling option is made somewhat easier for the parents of accelerated children by the proliferation of on-line resources for the gifted. Several universities offer distance-learning curriculums specifically for academically accelerated children. Correspondence courses are available from Stanford and Johns Hopkins universities, among others. A special school for gifted children in Australia offers an entire on-line curricu-lum. While these resources may be of interest mostly to parents trying to home-school, they also provide options for parents looking for extra enrichment activities to augment a public or private school's standard curriculum. For links to these and other related resources, try the GT World home page.[4] The Gifted and Talented Home Page also sponsors a pen-pal pro-gram specifically for children, labeled as "gifted" by their home schools, who want to exchange letters with another gifted child.

Universities have a vested interest in making contact with the scholars of tomorrow. In addition to the correspondence courses mentioned above, numerous universities sponsor sum-mer "talent searches," inviting children from all over the coun-try to attend a program of several weeks to meet other accelerated children, take short courses in an area of interest, and make contact with faculty. Financial aid is available to off-set some of the costs to the child's family. Such a summer experience can get a bored, cynical child excited about learning again, and it can also reward efforts made during the school year. While most of these programs, like the correspondence courses, are targeted to youngsters in the sixth grade and up, some solicit applications from younger children as well. Carnegie Mellon University in Pittsburgh, for example, offers a summer program for children as young as third graders, and the Graduate School of Education at the University of California at Berkeley's Academic Talent Development Program targets children as young as kindergarten age.[5]

## Select an Educational Plan and Run with It

Investigating options can be fun, but at some point you and your child will need to agree on a plan, at least for one school year at a time. No plan will be perfect, and no placement can prevent your child from being bored, restless, and impatient some of the time. This is just part of life. We have all experienced having to go slow when we would prefer to go fast. While you have been your child's ally through the process of choosing the best available option(s), it is wise to now remind your child that every setting has its difficulties. Every job involves a certain amount of boring, repetitive work, and school is no exception. Expect your child to do well in the educational setting you have chosen.

## Enrich the After-School Hours

To make school success more likely, and to balance work and play, try to arrange enriching activities for your child outside of school as well as in the formal learning situation. These should be activities you also enjoy. Accelerated children tend to crave variety and stimulation, and it works out well for everyone if they can find some of that in the company of a beloved parent. These activities need not be educational in any traditional sense; they should simply be fun and interesting for both you and your child. Here are some ideas to try:

- Put together a scrapbook of photos, mementos, and written comments to commemorate special family times.
- Cook a meal or snack together, perhaps learning a new cuisine from another part of the world.
- Explore museums, galleries, and bookstores.
- Explore local parks.
- Start a garden from scratch and keep a record of its progress.
- Pursue mutually enjoyable art and music activities.

Academically accelerated children were often read to as young children, and this is a family ritual that need not disappear as the child grows. Throughout elementary school, children still enjoy having a parent read aloud a more advanced book, one they cannot yet read themselves. Once they can read everything you can read, let the child read out loud to you from his or her current favorite book.

Such rewarding activities strengthen the bond between parent and child, which helps keep a bright child out of trouble. Activities also keep the youngster busy, so that school need not bear the entire burden of feeding this intellectually hungry consumer.

It is also important to guard against your child's turning into a "human brain," as opposed to a whole person. While other parents must insist that homework be completed, parents of accelerated children often find they have to insist that the child leave off schoolwork for a while and spend some daylight time outdoors. Physical exercise provides a necessary balance, and will help the child be more relaxed in school the next day.

## Family Activity

Read Stephanie Tolan's powerful essay, "Is It a Cheetah?" You can access this directly by going to www.stephanietolan.com/is_it_a_cheetah.htm, but if this link is hard to open (I have found it frequently is), you can also go into hoagiesgifted.org, click on "Readings," and click on "Stephanie Tolan" from there. Read aloud or have your older children read the essay and discuss it with them. Has anyone in your family ever felt rejected because of being different? Has school ever felt like a cage? What other kinds of differences, besides being on a different developmental trajectory, might make someone feel like a cheetah cub in lion country?

Finally, it is most important to guard against your child's self-esteem being tied to his or her superior academic abilities. While it may not happen yet, someday it will happen that the child will encounter peers who are better prepared or more talented—yes, even in his or her "special" areas. Very few of us get through life without serious competition. Teach your child that while it is important to do her best, how much she achieves is a contest with herself, not with others. Praise your child now and then for qualities other than academic abilities, and make sure to praise other children as well. Perhaps your child's friend Johnny is having trouble reading, whereas your kid is way ahead of the rest of the class in this area. Point out to your child that Johnny is very good at running races. The idea is to stress that every person has unique abilities and talents, that none of us is good at everything, and that we can notice and praise everyone's diverse talents. This will help your child learn, by imitating you, to get along with others in a world where everyone is different. (The discussion in Chapter 3 of multiple intelligences may be a useful notion in this regard.)

If your child feels too different, perhaps because of being singled out for a special class, keep stressing individual differences but try teaching your child some simple verbal self-defense skills as well. If Mary teases her about being a "brain," perhaps she can lightly tease back about Mary's being a cheerleader or a hall monitor. While your child *is* different from the norm, you don't want her to be either ashamed of this difference or too proud of it. Teach your child to value everyone's gifts, including her own. Making pen pals of other children across the country, also placed in special programs, is another way to lessen the accelerated child's uncomfortable sense of difference.[6]

---

## TEACHER TIPS

Here are strategies for working with your child's teachers—as they work with your challenging, curious child.

### Plan for Spare Time
Intellectually gifted children have to learn how to keep themselves busy; this is a skill they will need throughout

life. While it is certainly important to make sure that your child is given challenging work, strategize also about what to do when that work is done. There will almost certainly be times when your child has to wait for the rest of the class to catch up. During that time, your child might try reading a library book or writing an ongoing journal of thoughts, feelings, and observations (one gifted sixth grader calls this reaching in her "imagination pocket" for something to keep her busy).

Get permission in advance for these boredom-busting strategies. Unless you have discussed them in advance, your child may get in trouble for pulling out a library book during math time. By strategizing with the teacher, you may come up with more ideas for constructively keeping busy than you and your child could on your own.

### Encourage Your Child to Help Others

Educational research suggests it is usually best if it is arranged for your child to go into another classroom of younger students to do formal tutoring, both to maximize the experience and to avoid resentment from peers. However, I've found it helps classmates see Mr. Gifted/Talented as helpful and human, not just "different," if they can come to him with questions now and then, too. Check with your child's teachers about trying both kinds of experiences.

One gifted child I know regularly leaves his third-grade class and walks down the hall to a kindergarten class, where he reads aloud to the younger children—with great drama and enthusiasm. This required some coordination between the two classrooms' teachers, but it is the high point of this child's day—and great for the kindergarten children, too.

## Motivate Your Teacher

Once you've chosen an educational plan, you will want to check back with your child's teacher from time to time to see how things are progressing. This will work best if you salt the call with a little well-chosen praise. It helps to say something like "Johnny loves your class when it's project time" or "Mary learned so much from that Reader's Theater you did"; Johnny and Mary are more likely this way to keep getting pleasantly challenged, even when that means extra work for the teacher. Accelerated children are demanding, as you know from living with one at home, and they don't always notice how hard the teacher is trying—it helps if you can notice for them. Everyone remembers that story about Einstein flunking his fourth-grade math class; consider that it can't have been easy trying to be Einstein's math teacher!

## Look for Specialists in Gifted Education

Recognize that your child will be challenging, frustrating, demanding—and a lot of work for most of his teachers. He may also be wonderfully rewarding. Keep looking for a teacher who genuinely delights in your child's giftedness; finding the best match between teacher and child can be simply a matter of personality and luck. Nevertheless, you can increase your chances for a good match if you can get your child into a special-education program staffed by teachers who have taken the time and trouble to become certified as specialists in gifted education. This, in my view, is the optimal situation for accelerated children.

# Resources

Parents of children who are considered gifted intellectually tend to band together, perhaps more than any other group of parents. Interestingly, they often perceive a need to defend their children to some extent from the outside world, as Stephanie Tolan comments in her article (famous among parents of accelerated children) "Is It a Cheetah?" In it, she makes the strong metaphorical statement, "Lions kill cheetah cubs. They don't eat them, they just kill them. . . . Highly gifted children and their families often feel like cheetahs living in lion country."

The best way to explore the world of intellectually accelerated children and their families these days may be through the on-line communities that have evolved specifically for this population. Through this avenue you can experience a sense of camaraderie and also understand that these are parents who often feel their children are misunderstood. The best on-line sites to try are Hoagie's Gifted and Talented Page (www.hoagiesgifted.org), Gifted and Talented World (www.gtworld.org), the Gifted and Talented Resources Home Page (www.tagfam.org), and Britesparks (www.britesparks.com). All these sites have ways for parents to communicate with each other. The focus is on support for the parents as they advocate for their unusual children.

# 5

# "I Get So Frustrated!"

## *The Confused Child*

Lucy's parents have been very proud of her great start in school. Lucy started reading books back in kindergarten. In first grade, she read at the level of or ahead of the other children. True, by the end of first grade, her progress seemed to be slowing down a little, but still, her parents never anticipated the conversation they are now having with her fourth-grade teacher.

"Lucy is really not reading at grade level," the teacher reports. "I think we will have to either give her some special help or hold her back."

Lucy's father is very angry. "I told you this would happen if we let her watch too much television!" he snaps at his wife. "Lucy has gotten lazy about her reading now." Lucy will definitely hear about how displeased her parents are when they get home.

Mario, a middle school student, usually makes C's in his English class. He seems to know the material, but his writing skills are not good. He misspells a lot of words, and his sentences are short and clumsy. This week, though, Mario turned in a flawless book report. It is beyond the required length and has no spelling or grammatical errors, and the writing flows gracefully, very different from Mario's usual writing style.

His teacher is pretty sure she knows what happened. "You copied this off the Internet, didn't you?" she angrily confronts Mario. Mario stammers a protest, but can't explain except to lamely say, "It worked better because I got to type it this time." Mario's teacher scoffs at his excuse, and he gets an F for the report.

Constance has been getting A's and B's all through elementary and middle school. She is anxious to do well in high school, too. So when her civics teacher gives out a written memo describing the report due in six weeks, Constance raises her hand right away. "I don't quite understand this," she begins. "Could you go over it?"

"All the instructions are there in the memo," her teacher responds. "This is high school, and you should be able to read and follow instructions on your own." Some of the other students titter, and Constance, embarrassed, drops her question. When she gets home and tries to figure out the report assignment, though, no matter how many times she reads over the memo, she can't form a clear mental picture of what the teacher wants.

"There must be something wrong with me," she thinks. "I'm always so stupid about written instructions." She feels a familiar panic rising inside her.

Lucy, Mario, and Constance have relatively common types of learning problems. To have such a learning problem, which at times may rise to the level of an actual learning disability, is to live in an angry world. It is difficult for such a child to convince parents or teachers that there really is a problem. After all, adults may reason, the child did fine in earlier grades (or in other contexts or on a test in the same subject last week), so why should he have difficulty now? It is easy to decide that the child is simply lazy or defiant, and to interpret the child's own explanations as excuses.

This reaction, indeed, is what usually happens, and the result is a child who withdraws from adults and tries frantically to hide the problem. Immense frustration is felt by all involved, yet this frustration could have been so easily prevented if the learning problem were only identified.

Fortunately, learning problems are easier to spot once you know what you're looking for. Lucy's reading problem is by far the most common type, and could be more accurately described as a glitch in the educational system, for which parents usually must compensate. Mario has a more classic type of learning disability: *dysgraphia* (difficulty with manual handwriting). Like other classic learning disabilities, dysgraphia may be compensated for with available technology. Classic learning disabilities will be identified and discussed later in this chapter. Constance has a strong preference for one type of learning "channel"— one way to receive information—in her case, the auditory channel. People of any age who strongly prefer a particular learning channel find themselves disadvantaged when that avenue is not available to them. This is difficult to change, but can be ameliorated with specific commonsense strategies as well as with appropriate technology.

## Reading: The Most Common Problem

Let's start with Lucy's situation, an example of the most common type of learning difficulty in the United States—a difficulty with reading. This is frequently, though not always, diagnosed as *dyslexia*, which is simply a word construct from the Latin for "difficulty with" (*dys-*) "reading" (*lexia*). In 1998 the results of the National Assessment of Educational Progress (NAEP), a standardized nationwide examination, revealed that 38 percent of America's fourth graders cannot read at all—not even a simple sentence.[1] Unfortunately, this is not a new problem. Average reading scores in the United States have not changed significantly since 1971, when the NAEP assessed the average reading skills of children aged 9, 13, and 17 at a collective D− grade level.[2] Most at risk are children for whom English is a second language and children who speak a dialect rather than standard English. But the problem cuts across all groups and socioeconomic levels.

Many of these children are like Lucy: that is, they seem at first to progress well and may even astound their parents with apparent early reading in preschool and kindergarten, but then they fall behind. The grim outlook is that children who cannot read *fluently* by the end of the third grade will most likely never read with ease unless something changes in how they are instructed.[3] (By "fluently" I mean easy comprehension of age-appropriate texts as well as the ability to sound out unfamiliar words and make some sense of even those texts above the child's expected reading level.) Lucy and others like her cannot read fluently because they have learned to read by memorizing words. This strategy works fine at first, given the repetitive vocabulary of most early reading primers and the large illustrations that enable the reader to guess at what's coming. The child with a good memory may even seem precocious. But as the complexity of the assigned reading increases, it becomes painfully clear that students like Lucy have not truly learned to read at all.

# How Could This Happen?

The culprit here is the exclusive use of the *whole-language method* of reading instruction. Some children—possibly even a majority of children—will learn to read on their own if they are simply exposed to books, read to, and encouraged. This is the theory behind whole-language reading instruction. As one advocate puts it, "Have faith in children as learners. They can and usually will develop a grasp of letter/sound relationships with little direct instruction, just as they learned to talk without direct instruction."[4] This analogy, between learning to read and learning to speak, runs throughout the whole-language literature.

Initially it sounds quite plausible. However, like many another plausible theory, it doesn't work so smoothly in practice. For some children—that 40 percent who are not catching on to reading by the fourth grade—it clearly does not work at all. These children seem to need direct, explicit instruction in phonics—the relationship between letters, sounds, and words. It is certainly true that children need little direct instruction to learn to talk. Humans seem to have an innate predisposition to speak (often too much!). All children, in all cultures, who are neurologically healthy and able to hear will eventually speak. But all children in all cultures do not learn to read. In fact, most human societies have been largely illiterate. Indeed, at least for many people, reading seems to be a skill that *requires* direct instruction.

This simple truth has unfortunately become mired in political complexity. The whole-language method of reading instruction has been used in the United States, to a greater and lesser extent, since the turn of the century. It has always enjoyed great popularity in schools of education, where teachers are trained. There has been little room for genuine difference of opinion regarding the theory's utility. Only recently has definitive research emerged to demonstrate that direct teaching of phonics is essential.

In the late 1980s California's State Board of Education endorsed the whole-language method, which was then promoted throughout the state's elementary schools. In 1997, however, statewide evaluations showed that a majority of California's schoolchildren were reading below grade level and that California now ranked dead last—in a tie with Louisiana—in overall reading scores by state.[5] The California board angrily reversed its policy. Phonics was declared the method of choice in California schools. Wisconsin, Ohio, Washington, Oregon, Texas, North Carolina, and Georgia have all followed suit since 1997 and passed laws recommending phonics instruction. In addition, numerous candidates for office and several governors have rushed to endorse phonics.

Teachers have understandably bristled at lawmakers, whom they see as comparatively ignorant of educational issues, dictating how they should teach. Furthermore, most educators teaching today were trained exclusively in the whole-language method of reading instruction and may not know how to implement another approach. Many parents have lined up on one side or the other of the issue, depending on which candidates for office they support. This is unfortunate, for this should truly not be a political issue. Research in other areas of human behavior is often suggestive, rather than compelling; humans are complicated creatures, and absolutes are hard to come by. But research in the area of reading instruction is an exception. A large body of independent research overwhelmingly supports the phonics method and is so compelling that it should convince us all, regardless of party or faction.

Back in 1965, the National Institute of Childhood Health and Human Development (NICHD), an arm of the National Institutes of Health, quietly began a thirty-five-year, $200-million research project involving eighteen universities, including Harvard, Yale, Johns Hopkins, the University of Houston (Texas), and Florida State University. (The last two schools are significant because Texas and Florida have school systems with large numbers of children who do not know English as their first language—and who have special difficulties with reading.) Early findings from this series of studies first began to make their way into print in the late 1990s, and the final report was released in April 2000. This report unequivocally states that 85 to 90 percent of children now experiencing reading difficulties can overcome them with direct instruction in phonics.[6]

Think about these figures for a moment. If there were a breakfast cereal on the market that could claim to cure or prevent 90 percent of all children's' reading problems, with independent research from eighteen universities over a thirty-five-year period to back up this claim, wouldn't every parent in America be buying that cereal? When these findings percolate through the educational system, the phonics method will be just as "hot" as that cereal. The report does acknowledge that many whole-language activities, like reading aloud to children in the classroom, are also beneficial, but it stresses that direct, explicit instruction in phonics should be given equal weight and should begin in kindergarten. This will be a big change. Change takes time, of course, and, as we noted earlier, children who don't learn to read fluently by the end of the third grade are behind and at risk for dropping out later on.

*Direct, explicit phonics instruction*, the phrase used in the NICHD report, means that children are given assignments (usually worksheets) to demonstrate the relationship between sounds and letters. An example would be a worksheet that identifies the *c* sound as usually sounding like "kuh" and gives examples of *c* words, such as cat, car, cab. This would be accompanied by other worksheets explaining the *a* and *t* sounds. Only after the child had been drilled in these letter-sound relationships would the child be asked to put the *c*, *a*, and *t* sounds together and to sound out the word *cat*.

If you discuss this with your child's teacher, he or she may defensively protest that this kind of drill is boring to children. Remember that this is how most teachers were trained. Your child's teacher is not being difficult; she's just telling you what she learned. However it now appears that such repetition is not particularly boring to children in the early grades—in fact, they thrive on it. Any parent who has had to read a favorite book over and over and still heard a young child's request "Again!" can easily believe this. It is boring to adults, but that is not the same thing, is it?

The teacher may also state that phonics is taught in the classroom, saying she points to words as she reads them aloud or allows the children to look at alphabet books. This is effective for many children, it seems, but for that almost 40 percent of schoolchildren with reading problems, it's not enough. Direct, specific, and repeated instruction in the relationship between letters and sounds is needed.

## What You Can Do

If your child's reading performance is uneven or inconsistent, or if it worsens instead of improves as time goes on, check to see if your child is learning to read phonetically. This is something you can ascertain yourself. In an encouraging, playful way, ask your child to read a text above her usual reading level—perhaps a book you're reading or a magazine article. Notice how your child approaches individual words. If she attempts to sound out unfamiliar words (for example, reads "exit" as "x-it" or "eggs-ut"), then she is reading phonetically, even if she mispronounces certain words. If she cannot even guess at unfamiliar words, or guesses from the illustrations and the words around the word (for example, reads "exit" as "door"), she is "reading" by guessing and memorizing. Don't scold your child for this, as it simply reflects how she has been taught, but do get the child some basic drilling in phonics. Another simple test, for an older child, uses the popular Harry Potter books. These books abound with made-up words, like "Quidditch" and "dementors." Tell your child you don't know one of these words and ask for his help in sounding it out. Ask him how he knew to say the word that way. If he can explain the relationship between sounds and letters ("You say Kw to start because that's the sound Q makes"), he has the basic phonetic understanding he needs to read. Remember, though, that most teachers are still trained in the whole-language method, so don't be shy about seeking phonics instruction for your child.[7]

If it seems needed, provide or arrange for extra drill in phonics. By all means make your child's teacher aware of the most recent research, and encourage the school to build in basic instruction in phonics. But change in large systems takes time, and unlimited time is something you don't have if your child is having reading problems. NICHD studies found that even children in the fourth and fifth grades, already labeled as "severely dyslexic" and in special-education classes, could leap up one-and-a-half grade levels in only two months, given "extra" or supplementary phonics instruction.[8] These children continued to make steady progress even after the extra instruction was discontinued. So a few months of extra effort on your part might make a big difference. Don't expect nearly two years' gain in two months, though: the researchers drilled these children two hours a day, five days a week, and few parents would be up to that. Still, the fact that they were able to effect such dramatic changes even in older children whose problems were deemed "chronic" is very encouraging.

There are a variety of tools on the market to help parents supplement their children's phonics learning. Businesses have capitalized on the desperation parents feel when their child is not learning to read or seems to be going backward. The two most widely advertised products on the market, "Hooked on Phonics" and "The Phonics Game," have been shown by independent research to be effective *if* used with a parent.[9] But this is an important "if." What seems to help with phonics is the direct instruction, and that means an adult sitting with the child and talking about the sound-letter relationship; the materials alone are not enough. These heavily advertised materials are expensive, too, and parents may have as good results with a simple, inexpensive pack of phonics flash cards or a workbook (available at any educational supply store).

Another option for families with a personal computer is phonics-related software, and there is a plethora of those programs. Be sure, however, that whatever you purchase provides drill on the letter-sound relationship, rather than just teaching the alphabet or animating popular children's books. And, as with the games and workbooks, the parent needs to participate. Davidson's "Kid Phonics" software includes a simple game that tests the child's ability to hear the difference between phonemes (letters that stand for sounds), which may be especially useful if you suspect a hearing discrimination problem or if you speak English with an accent or in a dialect. My own child, for example, had difficulty hearing the difference between the vowel sounds in *pen* and in *pin*—because, with my Texas accent, I have trouble pronouncing the difference! Consult your budget, your and your child's learning preferences (Do you like to play games on the computer? Does your child gravitate to brightly colored workbooks with reward stickers?), and try out some materials.

The most important rules to follow are to make this phonics drill fun and not punitive, to stop when the child has had enough, and to commit to at least a little practice five days a week until you see improvement. If your schedule does not permit this, or if you get too frustrated and impatient with your child when you try it, you may want to consider hiring a professional tutor. The popular Fast Forward program is a phonics-tutoring program that can be brought into a school (by arrangement with the principal) or contracted for an individual child with a private provider (listed by area). Reading Recovery is another such program, so far available only to schools. The Score and Kumon after-school tutoring franchises use phonics instruction as well. Some independent, individual tutors in your area can be located through the website www.tutor .com. Whether franchise or independent, be sure to specify to your child's tutor that you want explicit instruction in phonics.

# If Your Child Needs More

Current research results indicate that much of what was previously thought to be dyslexia is actually difficulty with phonics, a difficulty that can be ameliorated by drill. It was formerly thought that dyslexic children have difficulty seeing letters, as they frequently reverse letters and words in writing. But it is now thought that this lack of clarity relates to their not understanding the letter-sound relationship, so the order isn't obvious to them. Even if your child has been diagnosed as "severely

## From a Former Confused Child

Hannah is a forty-year-old full-time homemaker who loves to read and volunteers as a reader at her local library. When helping her own children in school, she realized recently that she could have been diagnosed with a learning disability back when she was in school, had she known how to describe her frustrations. Here's how she describes discovering she was learning disabled.

"I had no idea that's what I was. I thought I was just stupid. Everyone else learned to read in the first grade, but I was still struggling. I was nearsighted and I could barely see those little words, and it was too hard to memorize them all. Finally my grandmother took me aside and drilled me on the sounds all the letters make. She gave me a book she had when she was a girl back in Kentucky, and it had some phonics worksheets in it. I practiced over and over, and I was so proud the day I could go back into second grade and really read.

"After that, I could read everything. I went from being one of the lowest readers to being in the top reading group. They don't say which group is the top, of course, but we all knew: the 'sparrows'—those were the dummies, like I used to be—and the 'robins'—that's the group I got to be in once I knew the secret. That was how I thought of it, a secret code, the secret of reading, only I could never figure out how come they didn't just teach it to us. You had to kind of figure it out on your own.

"After that I thought I was smart, for a while. Then in third grade we had to learn how to draw maps. I drew a bunch of maps, but then the teacher asked me which way was north in my maps. I thought north was always straight ahead, that it was just the word for going straight ahead, and I said so. The class roared with laughter, and I was mortified. I never got better than a C on a map. But I didn't really ask after that one time or try to see what the problem was. I figured I better just lay low until the unit on maps was over.

"Now I realize I have a kind of block against visual-spatial information. I had a terrible time in geometry, too, later on, though I loved algebra, which is a kind of language. I had to give up my dream of becoming a nurse because I couldn't pass organic chemistry. I thought I was just too dumb, but I found out later that organic chemistry requires visual-spatial skills again. I bet the same thing caused my early trouble with reading. I bet I had trouble and had to have the phonics explained to me because I couldn't memorize the words just from seeing them. I couldn't even see that well, period. I wish now, someone had told me there is a name for what I couldn't do. Maybe there would have been a way to help. As it was, I just kept my head down and avoided certain subjects.

"It's not really a problem in my adult life. I found the work I love, I have a family, and everyone who knows me just knows—don't ask Hannah to draw a map or find her way to a new place by herself. I'm just Hannah, the dumb one at directions. It's just who I am by now. And at least I learned to read, right?"

dyslexic," try the phonics suggestions you have just read about, with a professional tutor if need be, before accepting the diagnosis.

However, for a smaller percentage of children (an estimated 20 percent of those diagnosed with dyslexia), drill in phonics does not seem to be enough to ensure their reading ability.[10] These children most probably have some kind of perceptual difficulty that makes it more difficult for them to hear the differences between phonemes. You should have your child checked for actual vision or hearing difficulties if there has been a diagnosis of dyslexia. If extra drill in phonics is not helping and tests show no discernible hearing or vision problems, your child may need special instruction to build up her area of weakness—and may benefit from assistive technology.

The situation is the same with the less commonly diagnosed, but equally disabling, *dysgraphia* and *dyscalculia*. The *dys-*, once again, means "difficulty with"; dysgraphia means difficulty writing by hand, and dyscalculia means difficulty with simple mathematical calculations, such as addition and subtraction. If vision and hearing tests rule out any problem in those areas and extra drills don't seem to help, you are left with the classic "learning disability." In these cases, the origins are uncertain (although often associated with premature birth, birth traumas, and early-childhood infections), and the outcome of remediation is not completely predictable.

With classic disabilities, though, there are steps you can take.

## Try to Get a Formal Diagnosis

It will be easier to get your child special instruction with a learning specialist, and permission for him to use compensatory technology, if he has an official diagnosis of learning disability. In most schools, this designation means the child must be at least two years behind grade level. Learning disabilities can be diagnosed only by inference, and they are not easy to establish. It helps to review your child's homework and class work yourself. If you find uneven performance (for example, Mario's excellent book report the one time he was not asked to write the report by hand), collect examples of it. What you are looking for is the exception that proves that your child can do better work when his area of weakness is bypassed.

A psychologist can administer an intelligence test and look for discrepancies, particularly among subsets of abilities or between verbal and performance measures. (Verbal skills involve talking, reading, and writing, whereas performance skills—like solving puzzles and reading maps—do not.) Organizations with a special interest in learning disabilities sponsor some on-line tests.[11] By law, any professional with a master's degree in education can diagnose a learning disability, so you may have most success working with a sympathetic teacher or learning specialist (also called an exceptional-education teacher or, at a higher level, exceptional-education coordinator), especially if you can show examples from the child's work. If you can prove the diagnosis, you are more likely to get specialized help in the public schools.

## Ask Specifically for What You Want

Even if you cannot get a formal diagnosis, it is worthwhile to ask for what you would like for your child. Many teachers are willing to cooperate, within certain limits, based on the homework and class work evidence you present.

- **Don't ask for a separate classroom.** Your child will have to compete with others who do not have this learning disability all his life. It is not to his advantage to segregate him from the rest of the class full-time.
- **Do ask for extra help.** Rather than simply drilling the child on the same material presented in the classroom, a learning specialist focuses on remediating the child's area of weakness. For example, children with difficulty distinguishing letters

may be asked to write letters in sand over and over to better grasp the differences. Children who have difficulty with the act of writing may practice pencil strokes and strokes with a paintbrush. Children who aren't grasping the concept of addition may be given a group of actual objects to move around, add to, and subtract from. Such activities can be done by the classroom teacher, too, if there is time or by an aide, under the guidance of a learning specialist. The parent can also try some of these activities at home. The goal is to try different ways to build up the child's area of weakness.

• **Do seek permission to use technology.** A disability of this kind may never be completely overcome, but it can be compensated for to an increasing extent, thanks to modern technology.[12] Children who have difficulty reading texts often do better reading a computer screen, on which the letters can be made easier to distinguish. On the monitor screen, the letters can easily be magnified several times over, for example. In addition, getting books on tape and taping lecture notes to play back later can reduce the child's overall reading load. Children like Mario, with writing problems, may do much better work when relieved of the manual tedium of writing and allowed use of a word processor. Newer voice-recognition software makes creative writing much easier for them, as they can develop a rough draft orally and then correct the text on the word processor. And a calculator can make it possible for a child with dyscalculia to progress to higher levels of mathematics, even algebra and calculus.

Albert Einstein reportedly didn't know his own phone number; when people remarked on this, he is said to have remarked loftily, "I never waste space in my brain for anything that can be written down instead." It seems likely he had some form of learning disability involving rote memorization of numbers—

perhaps another reason he failed fourth-grade math. This problem obviously did not hold him back, and such difficulties need not hold your child back, either, now that the technology to address them is so widely available.

Especially in the early grades, however, a formal diagnosis (or at least a letter from a physician) may be needed to get permission for your child to use assistive devices, such as laptop computers, tape recorders, and calculators. Later on, permission is easier to come by in school, as the emphasis is more on higher-level skills than on such basics as manual handwriting, addition, and the like. Even in elementary school you can ask if your child may be permitted to use technology on at least some assignments, even if you can't get permission for all of them. This way you and your child can see firsthand if the assignment is easier to complete—and how much easier it is— when this technology is provided, and the teacher can see the child's true abilities when the disability is out of the way.

If you are successful in getting a formal diagnosis, with testing from a psychologist, with the support of a learning specialist, or with the evidence you yourself collect (or by using all three avenues), the school is not only required to permit the use of such devices but also to purchase them for your child (under the IDEA provisions). If you know this would be a hardship for your public school, you may be able to use this information as a bargaining chip: for example, you might argue, "I won't ask the school to buy the laptop right away if I can just get permission for my son to try one out in class." But you can and should insist on the school administrator's arranging for at least the loan of such devices if they are beyond your means and your child really needs them.

Another option is to check out your health-care provider to see if assistive devices are covered under your insurance plan, with a letter from a physician confirming the learning-disability diagnosis. Medicare and Medicaid will usually pay, although private insurance companies differ on coverage. Xerox Adaptive Technologies and Franklin Learning Resources are two full lines of assistive devices, ranging from expensive, complex word-processing and book-scanning systems to simple, inexpensive voice-activated calculators, all specifically targeted to persons with learning disabilities.[13]

## Be Persistent in Asking

This area is definitely a case of the squeaky wheel's getting the grease. The public school system may be most responsive, but a small private school may also be willing to comply with your wishes if you can specify exactly what you need and are willing to bring in your own assistive devices. I generally do not recommend home schooling for a child with a classic learning disability—it is too easy for parent and child to become frustrated with each other about the learning differences. An exception, though, is the situation where the parent has the same disability as the child, and has learned to work around it. The parent is then well placed to coach the child on what has worked.

## Get Support from Other Parents

There is a large and active community of parents whose children have been diagnosed with or suspected of having learning disabilities. Keeping in touch with other parents[14] can help you stay positive and active in asking for what your child needs. Be aware, however, that you will get many suggestions for every problem. You'll have to be critical in your evaluation—ask to see research results before jumping into every program another parent recommends. Remember that glowing testimonials are not research evidence, particularly when there has been no control group or follow-up evaluations.

## Broaden Your Perspective

In a sense, we all have learning disabilities—some areas of learning that are more difficult for us than others. Some of us are lucky in that our particular disability (two left feet when it comes to dancing, no ear for music, poor spelling skills) didn't handicap us as much in school as some other types of weak areas (difficulties with reading and basic math, for example). Over time, most people learn to work around whatever areas of strength and areas of weakness they have. There is every reason to believe your child will do the same, especially with the encouraging new technology being developed every day.

## Developmental Optometry

If your child has any difficulty that might involve vision (and this certainly includes dyslexia, dysgraphia, and dyscalculia), you will want to arrange for thorough eye evaluations. But even if your child's vision is completely 20/20, there is another option to consider as well. Some developmental optometrists offer visual-perceptual training, which, they claim, produces impressive results. This training can help children who have difficulty in reading or mathematics to better perceive letters, mathematical symbols, and the like. The developmental optometrists contend that these difficulties may be caused by deficiencies in visual coordination, and they offer a graduated series of vision exercises. Their work remains controversial, and other professionals have expressed skepticism. But if your child has chronic difficulty distinguishing letters or symbols (for example, she adds when she's supposed to subtract; he confuses directions), you may be interested in exploring this idea. Parents Active for Vision Education can give you information on how to locate a properly trained developmental optometrist (with postgraduate training in this type of therapy) and on whether your health insurance covers this type of treatment.[15] If your child has had crossed eyes, squints frequently, experiences blurred vision when trying to do schoolwork, or characteristically tilts his head or closes one eye when reading, this is an important option for you to consider.

## Learning Channels

The Smith family is assembling a tricycle for its youngest family member, little Sally. It is Christmas Eve, and tempers are fraying. Bob Smith, Sally's father, is on the phone, talking to a harried sales clerk trying to leave the store. "Can't you just explain to me how to put this thing together?" he is asking. "Bob!" snaps Janet, his wife. "Why are you talking to that guy? The instructions are right here, and all we have to do is read them. I just wish they were written more clearly." Meanwhile, Jim, the Smith's teenage son and Sally's older brother, is ignoring both parents and experimenting with trying to attach the wheels first one way, then another.

To Janet, both Bob and Jim seem to be ignoring the obviously "right" way to figure out how to put the tricycle together. Janet prefers learning information in a visual-verbal way, and she can be a little self-righteous about this; her preference, reinforced throughout school, is the one most people in our culture hold. But many other people, like Bob, prefer to learn using the auditory channel, having someone give the explanation to them out loud. And a smaller but still significant number, like Jim, prefer to learn in a kinesthetic way—through actual hands-on trial and error. All three Smiths have been ignoring the diagram that accompanies the written instructions. A diagram or map is most useful to people who prefer to learn in a visual-spatial way. While only a relatively small number of people have this preference, most engineers indeed prefer the visual-spatial channel, so the engineer who designed the tricycle would be surprised to see that no one is using his lovely diagram.[16]

## Family Activity

Go to ldpride.net and click on their Learning Styles Exam. At this fun site there are no right and wrong answers, and it is interesting to compare how differently people within the same family receive and process information. Seeing these results can underline the point that we all have our individual areas of strength and of weakness.

Often these preferences for various learning methods are simply orientations causing no problems more serious than some miscommunication among the individuals working together on a common project. But at times, for certain people, the preference for one channel is so strong as to amount to a block against the other ways of receiving information. This is what happens with Constance—she so strongly prefers the auditory channel that it is hard for her to receive or absorb information given only in a visual-verbal form. This kind of strong preference may be associated with an actual perceptual difficulty or with relative strengths and deficits in brain functioning. It is thus classified as a learning disability. Whatever the cause, it is not easily changed.

So Constance should take a twofold approach. First, she can use exercises designed to improve her ability to access information visually-verbally. These exercises would play against her usual tendency to rely on auditory input. For example, she could watch her favorite movies with the sound turned off; she could write letters instead of talking on the phone. (Similarly, someone who usually relies on visual-verbal rather than auditory input might practice listening to books on tape with his eyes closed.) But it would be wise for Constance (in addition to trying to build up her ability in visual-verbal areas), second, to compensate for her weakness.

If you suspect your child may have a strong preference for one learning channel at the expense of others, or a block against another learning channel, here are ways you can help the child learn to compensate.

## Pay Attention to What Works

In Constance's case, it would be useful for her to remember that back in elementary and middle school, when she could get teachers to read the instructions out loud and discuss them with her, she had no difficulties. This is important so she can stay encouraged, and it also gives her an important aid in pinpointing what ways of processing information work well for her.

## Learn to Articulate What Works and What Is Difficult

It would have been helpful if Constance had known how to say to her high school teacher, perhaps privately after class, "I have difficulty processing visual-verbal information. Could we set up a time for me to ask you some questions regarding the assignment?" Her teacher might not have been any more responsive, but then again he might have understood better and helped more. Even more important, Constance could have reminded herself that the channel of information is what the problem is— and not that she is "stupid" or incompetent. So it is helpful to be able not only to pinpoint the problem but also to tell others, yourself, or your child what is going on.

Sometimes identifying what is a strength and what is a weakness is obvious; Constance, for instance, already knows she has trouble with written (visual-verbal) information. But if there are questions about a diagnosis or difficulty with learning, or if you wish to become familiar with the technical language of learning channels, there are several interesting, easy-to-take tests on-line to ascertain your learning preference (and how strong it is). [17]

## *Play to Your Strengths by Translating*

Simple as it seems, if Constance asks her mother or a friend to read the assignment out loud to her, she is likely to understand it much better. If she then tape-records herself or someone else explaining the assignment, and plays this back periodically as she works on it, she will have constructed a way of learning that works for her. Someone with difficulty attending to auditory information, on the other hand, who has a teacher who gives assignments out loud and then won't repeat them, will do well to take down what the teacher says, or tape-record it if possible, and then "translate" that into written instructions. Visual-spatial learners, in contrast, benefit from taking written information and trying to put it into graph or map form. (Mind mapping is a method of note taking that works particularly well for visual-spatial learners.[18]) Kinesthetic learners probably have the hardest time, as this method of learning is downplayed in

most schools, considered as being "too noisy," "too dangerous," or "too messy." A true kinesthetic learner is likely to do
better in an alternative private school setting, where such
options as using actual objects to explore math problems or
enacting characters in history instead of merely reading or hearing about them are both possible to carry out and encouraged.
When a kinesthetic learner must adapt to a verbal-visual presentation of material, as is usually the case in schools, he may
benefit from studying with a group of others who will allow
him to explore interactive ways of understanding the information. His creativity and enthusiastic hands-on approach, in turn,
may be novel and interesting to the others.

By sometime in high school it is useful for nearly everyone
to figure out their preferred learning channel and how to adapt
information to use that channel. Most college students waste a
lot of time studying by using methods not applicable to them.
For example, a student oriented to the auditory writes facts
over and over, then doesn't retain them for the exam; her
roommate, meanwhile, studies in a group, and tries to memorize answers by discussing them aloud, working against her
visual-verbal strength and also failing to retain the information.
An average to superior student can (perhaps) get away with
such wasteful methods of studying in high school, but in college and graduate school it becomes ever more important to
play to one's strengths. For some children, who have strongly
preferred learning channel(s) and blocks against other channels,
it may be crucial already at the elementary school level to realize what works best.

## Consider Assistive Technology

Technology can be a real asset, as it is with the classic learning
disabilities, to those with a weakness in one or more learning

channels. Youngsters who have difficulty absorbing visual-verbal information can use tape recorders rather than take notes, to play back instructions and to study. Further, when permitted, they can use books on tape, scanners, and voice recognition software to master some reading and writing assignments. Individuals who have had a diagnosis of a learning disability, which must be honored at the college as well as the elementary and secondary school levels, have a strong case to use these assistive devices.

Children who have difficulty understanding or using auditory information can use a transcription machine to turn a tape-recorded lecture into notes; they can try mind-mapping. Those who have trouble with visual-spatial information have no technology presently available to them—perhaps because most computer professionals are strongly visual-spatial! But, on the other hand, some carmakers are experimenting with built-in "talking maps," which would take visual-spatial information and translate it into verbal directions.

All learning problems and disabilities can usefully be seen in terms of relative strengths and relative weaknesses. We all have these, so we all learn a little differently. But when there is a marked area of weakness, the compensation must be more conscious and begin earlier. With basic building blocks of learning, such as the letter-sound connection in reading (phonics), repetitive drill helps build up an area of weakness. When this approach isn't working, other techniques may be tried, which allow the person to skip over the area of weakness and play to his or her strengths. Assistive technology can be a great help with utilizing alternative strengths. Later in life, and particularly once basic reading skills are established, playing to one's strengths is likely to be a more enjoyable and useful process than drill.

## TEACHER TIPS

These are some tips that may help you and your child to work with your teachers to compensate for or overcome areas of weakness in learning.

**Teach Your Child to Speak Up About Special Needs**
Throughout children's lives, they will benefit from being able to articulate what strategies work best for them. Some of the kids I teach are great about coming up to me in class and saying something like, "I know you said those vocabulary words in class, but I'll study better for the test if you could write them down also," or "I know the instructions are written here, but could you read them aloud for me?" I am happy to help out, even when the child is not formally classified as learning disabled.

**Take Your Child Along to Meet with the Teacher**
Scheduling a meeting with your child's teacher and including your child (even if she is only of elementary-school age) in the session is helpful. This helps the child begin to learn to talk about his learning differences. Children often have considerable insight into what helps them learn, and they'll tell us if we are willing to listen. From such meetings, they can also learn to give simple, concise descriptions of their learning challenges: "I learn best from what I hear, and written instructions don't always work for me," or "I have a hard time reading diagrams; could you explain this to me in words instead?" When setting up a reward system for improvement in school, completion of tasks, and so forth include recognition for speaking up and describing learning needs. If Hannah, who spoke about the difficulty she had learning to read and understand maps, had

been trained in this way, she would have known what kind of help to ask for in organic chemistry, and she might be able to find resources for translating maps into verbal directions.

### Ask About Available Resources

The Library of Congress provides books on tape to children with reading or visual disabilities. They have a wide selection, and the taped books will be mailed to the child's home, on loan, free of charge until the child is done "reading" them. It is also possible to rent scanners, word processors, tape recorders, and other technology free of charge for a child with special needs.

### Keep in Touch with the Teacher

A close partnership between school and home is most useful for children with special learning needs. These kids take extra time and care on a daily basis—daily notes, many meetings, constant modification. Stay involved, and let the teacher know you appreciate her involvement. It is critical to get the child through the early grades and well launched onto a viable career path. Along the way, the child will have to learn to balance healthy self-confidence with a realistic assessment of his own strengths and weaknesses. This will happen only if everyone—child, teacher, and parent—works together as a team.

# Resources

Here are additional resources related to the topics of children with special areas of learning weakness or difficulty.

## Websites

Parents of children diagnosed with learning disabilities, like those who have "accelerated" children, seem to feel a need for support from one another but even greater a need for resources that can bolster their children's self-esteem, too often lacerated by experiences of failure. So, in addition to offering parents the chance to exchange ideas and band together, the primary websites related to learning disabilities also focus on building the pride of individuals with learning differences. These primary sites are LD Online (www.ldonline.org), LD Pride (www.ldpride.net), and the Learning Disabilities Association of America (www.ldanatl.org). LD Online has an especially nice section in which children can display their artwork and stories, and features an extensive First Person Gallery, a collection of first-person stories told by individuals who have struggled with a learning disability. These can be very encouraging for young people; one of the First Person narrators is Paul Orfalea, the entrepreneur founder of Kinko's Copies, and there also are doctors, lawyers, and all sorts of professionals who realized their dreams in spite of early difficulties.

## Videos

Numerous books have been written on learning disabilities, but since difficulty with reading is so often part of the problem, you might instead try a series of professionally produced videos, *The Learning Project Videos*. The series focuses on increasing empathy and understanding about learning differences. The videos are suitable for older children, teens, and adults. They are available as a set or individually from Amazon.com, and for each video purchased, Amazon.com donates a percentage to LD Online.

# 6

# "I Can't Concentrate!"

## *The Inattentive Child*

The number of children in the United States diagnosed with attention-deficit hyperactivity disorder (ADHD) has grown exponentially in the last decade. Estimates are that between 5 and 10 percent of all U.S. children carry this diagnosis.[1] Even this percentage is probably low, as it is uncontrolled for income level, gender, and other variables. Indeed, one study of a school district in southeastern Virginia found that 20 percent of all fifth-grade boys were taking Ritalin for ADHD.[2]

One result of these diagnoses has been a corresponding exponential growth in debate and discussion about children who seem inattentive. Parents of children with other types of learning difficulties may feel alone with their problems. But parents whose children have difficulties paying attention typically receive more advice today than they could possibly want, much of it contradictory. If your child sometimes acts distracted, inattentive, fidgety, or hyperactive, you are likely to find yourself in the storm of controversy that swirls around the diagnosis of attention deficit disorder. To experience what that is like, let's follow Janet's attempts to make sense of the situation.

Janet is a realistic composite of many of my counseling clients. As you read about the passionate, confusing, and often strange-sounding advice she received, see if you can determine when she is hearing something completely false, and when her advisor is overstating, exaggerating perhaps, but nonetheless sharing with her at least a partial truth.

Janet's daughter, Ashley, is eight years old. A quiet, shy child, she does not present a behavior problem. So Janet is stunned when Ashley's third-grade teacher suggests, "You really should have your daughter evaluated for attention deficit disorder." True, Ashley's grades have been slipping for some time, she constantly has to be reminded what to do at home and at school, and she daydreams in class to the extent that she sometimes fails to hear important information. But Janet thought that Ritalin was for "hyperactive" children, like her friend's son who almost set fire to his house. Ashley's teacher, however, says that medication would be helpful for Ashley, too.

Janet agrees to have Ashley evaluated. The problem is that no one seems clear on who is most qualified to do this. Ashley's teacher says that from her years of experience in public schools she "knows" the signs of attention deficit disorder. Janet's usual pediatrician tells her right away that he doesn't know that much about ADHD, but he adds, "If Ashley's teacher wants to give medication a try, it couldn't hurt. Besides, we can use the medication to help us make the diagnosis. For children with attention deficit disorder, Ritalin and other such stimulants have a paradoxical effect—the stimulation actually calms them down and helps them focus. And that wouldn't work unless there was a genuine neurological imbalance."

This sounds reasonable to Janet. However, she would like a second opinion. But the school psychologist she calls tells her, "I can't prescribe medication or make this diagnosis myself. Your daughter should be seeing a child psychiatrist." And the child psychiatrist she calls tells her, "Have you taken the child to see her family doctor? A family doctor who knows the child is the best person to make the diagnosis." The guidance counselor at Ashley's school gives Janet some forms to fill out, asking how often Ashley is "distracted," "won't follow directions," and so on. Janet is confused. Why is she being asked to describe the problem—isn't that what the diagnosis is for?

Meanwhile, since Janet let slip that she was considering the teacher's suggestion, she has been getting bombarded with advice on all sides. Her mother calls long distance to say that she read an article about this, adding, "Children who take Ritalin are more likely to abuse drugs as teenagers. And it will stunt her growth, too!" On the other hand, Janet's next-door neighbor, who recently moved to this country from Canada, tells Janet, "I don't want to say anything against the schools here, but you just don't see this in Canada. Not like you do here. And my mother back in Great Britain, a schoolteacher for decades, tells me she's never had a child in her class on Ritalin. This is just some kind of strange American thing." Janet's best friend, Ellen, also has advice: "I told you this would happen if you took that promotion at work. This is because you're working too hard and are too busy when you do get home. What do you expect? The child needs more attention from you."

Wracked with guilt, and still uncertain about how to proceed, Janet mentions to Ashley's soccer coach that she wishes she knew some other parents who have decided to give their child Ritalin. The coach says he will ask around. When she gets home from work the next day, Janet already has six phone messages from soccer league parents. The phone messages are as follows:

"My child was failing school until my doctor put him on medication. Now he's a different child! He's much easier to live with at home, too. Don't waste any time—follow your doctor's advice on this. And, by the way, we have a support group you may want to attend—CHADD (that stands for Children and Adults with Attention Deficit Disorders)."

"Don't put your child on that terrible medication! It made my child so jittery and anxious he couldn't sleep. It's the school's fault. Reginald is much improved since we put him in Catholic school, where there's more structure and they have smaller classes."

"Our Gwendolyn has been much happier since we moved her to an alternative school, where she has more freedom and less structure. There's no need to medicate. Attention-deficit-disorder children are really warriors at heart—they just need room to explore and be creative. Let me tell you about our support group—Born to Explore, we call it."

"The answer is diet. Take Ashley off all processed foods and sugar. It's well known that attention deficit disorder is basically caused by diet. Just look at how hyper children get the day after Halloween, after they've eaten all that candy!"

"We tried the medicine but it didn't work for us. But Kevin is a changed child since we signed him up for karate lessons. And also he's been doing biofeedback, and we're getting him into that new interactive metronome program."

"Don't worry, she'll grow out of it."

By now Janet has a splitting headache. How can she tell who is giving her useful advice and who is passing on myths and misinformation? And why should there be so much controversy about this common diagnosis?

The advice Janet is getting is replete with partial truths and one-sided accounts. Yet only the reasonable-sounding pediatrician's statement is absolutely false. With that one exception, there is *some* truth behind everything Janet was told, however contradictory the statements seem. This illustrates the complex nature of the ADHD controversy.

# The ADHD Controversy

We know that increased numbers of children in the United States are viewed by their parents and teachers as having difficulty in paying attention. Most of these children are boys, but some, like Ashley, are girls (boys are diagnosed at a rate of 3:1 compared to girls). Boys (and some girls) diagnosed with ADHD are more likely to be physically active, boisterous, and difficult to control. They are said to have hyperactivity as well as attention deficit disorder. However, some girls with this diagnosis (and some quieter boys) may be no trouble in the classroom, although they appear to daydream, lose focus, and become unable to complete their work. They are said to have attention deficit disorder of the primarily inattentive type, without hyperactivity. Both types are referred to as ADHD in the most up-to-date psychiatric nomenclature.[3]

The number of children in the United States diagnosed with one form or another of attention deficit disorder today is five times greater than the number was in 1990. That figure has gone from 900,000 to more than 5 million individuals during one decade! During the same time period, there has been a 700 percent increase in the use of Ritalin, the most common drug prescribed for attention deficit disorder.[4] Janet's Canadian neighbor is right: this is almost entirely a phenomenon limited to the United States of America. The United States produces and consumes 90 percent of the world's entire supply of Ritalin.[5] In the United Kingdom, Canada, and Western Europe, the diagnosis of attention deficit disorder is much less common, and psychostimulants are not commonly prescribed to children. Elsewhere in the world, the condition is virtually unknown.

Theories abound as to causation. In the United States the most common medical viewpoint is that ADHD represents a brain dysfunction of some unknown origin.[6] Physicians who see ADHD in this way will treat the problem with psychostimulant medications, such as Ritalin (methylphenidate HCL), Adderall (mixed salts of an amphetamine product), and Dexedrine (dextroamphetamine sulfate).

At times, exposure to lead, actual brain injury, or problems in childbirth do predate a diagnosis of ADHD, lending credence to the brain-dysfunction hypothesis. That is not true, however, for the majority of children diagnosed with ADHD in the United States today. Some children diagnosed with ADHD have a thyroid problem, which, though rare, produces symptoms of ADHD in three out of four patients who have it.[7] Most ADHD children, however, show no detectable medical abnormalities.

In an attempt to locate some more widespread brain dysfunction, researchers have explored the possibility that individuals with ADHD process information in the frontal cortex somewhat differently than do the rest of us. The idea here is that ADHD individuals may become quickly overwhelmed when presented with too much information. The technique used to get images of the frontal cortex in action is still experimental, however, and the research results have been inconclusive. In 1998 the National Institutes of Health flatly stated that "After years of clinical research . . . our knowledge about the cause or causes of ADHD remains speculative."[8]

Nonetheless, medication remains a common treatment. For years, it was thought that Ritalin and other psychostimulants had a paradoxical effect particularly on children with ADHD, calming them down instead of speeding them up. So Janet's pediatrician was probably just repeating what he learned in medical school. However, more recent research has shown that, in fact, stimulants have a calming and focusing effect on everyone, child and adult alike.[9] The degree varies from individual to individual, but the effect is common to all, and thus cannot be, as was previously thought, a clue to diagnosis. If it seems strange that a stimulant would actually make it easier for you to concentrate, just think about caffeine. In overly strong doses, caffeine can make you jittery, sleepless, and anxious, and it is certainly a stimulant. Yet millions of adult Americans reach for that morning cup of coffee because they know it will actually help them concentrate at work. Ritalin and other stimulants, in moderation, have a somewhat similar effect, and they are popular on college campuses for this very reason. This certainly does not mean children should be taking strong stimulants indiscriminately; it simply means Ritalin might well improve Ashley's school performance, whether or not she has any kind of neurological deficit. So might a strong cup of black coffee every few hours during the school day.

But we typically don't give young children stimulants such as coffee, for fear of side effects. Side effects are also a concern with Ritalin. Like any stimulant, Ritalin and its psychostimulant cousins can decrease appetite. Diet pills also contain stimulants; the idea is that if you're all charged up, you will be less likely to stop and feel hungry. For growing children, that is not good news, as they need to eat to grow properly. As Ashley's grandmother somewhat too dramatically warned, in some cases a lack of appetite resulting from prescribed psychostimulants can actually reduce food consumption to the point that it inhibits a child's growth ("It will stunt her growth"). To guard against that, physicians prescribing such medications for children usually advise that the child pass the summer vacation from school off the medication, and possibly not take it during the weekends as well.

More subtly, Ashley might get the message that taking a pill is the way to solve her problems. Ashley's grandmother is also right that, statistically, teenagers taking psychostimulants for

ADHD are more likely to use other drugs illegally.[10] Why this spillover effect occurs is not known. It is quite possible that it is the impulsive behavior that so often accompanies inattentiveness—in other words, the behaviors for which the child is being treated, not the treatment—that prompts the illegal drug use. Nevertheless, the finding is worrisome. It is especially so because Ritalin and other stimulants have a street value—they can be resold illegally at a profit—and are in hot demand on college and high school campuses. This inevitably puts a teenager with a legitimate supply of Ritalin in a position of temptation, by ensuring that he will be approached by youngsters already involved with illegal drugs who hope to buy and resell his medications.

Later in the chapter we will discuss how to handle this problem if you do decide to try medication for your child. For now, let us just note that there are concerns about the increasingly widespread use of psychostimulants by children in the United States, and these concerns strongly motivate individuals who disagree with the biological view of ADHD.[11]

A second school of thought holds that the characteristic scanning, rapidly changing thoughts of a person who might be diagnosed with ADHD represent a valid evolutionary advantage.[12] This school speculates that perhaps, in times past, such restless thinking also characterized early hunters and warriors, unlike the stolid, plodding farmer type of person who may have an easier time in school. This theory appeals to many individuals who have been diagnosed with ADHD. By its nature, however, the notion is speculative and cannot be conclusively demonstrated.

Attentional differences can also be positively explained as differences in temperament, creativity, or simply as someone's "marching to the beat of a different drummer." One recent bestselling book even speculates that children who have ADHD symptoms may represent a new, more advanced human type (dubbed the Indigo Children), more adapted than the rest of us to life in a computerized world.[13] Indigo children are said to have great sensitivity but short attention spans, and their love for technology is matched only by their dislike of conventional authority (and school).

Finally, the third group of theorists consider that ADHD is a "fake" diagnosis, reflecting only our society's overly rapid pace and its tendency to turn to pharmaceuticals to solve problems.[14] Adherents of this view point to the rapid increase in the use of Ritalin in the United States alone and the lack of any clear biological causation. Although they don't wax as poetic about warriors and explorers as the second group, they are nonetheless more in sympathy than not with those who see individual differences in attention span as potentially positive. And they speculate about possible cultural ills unique to, or found in exaggerated form, within the United States, giving rise to a "culture of stimulation." Above all, they disapprove of placing large numbers of children on psychostimulant medication.

All three viewpoints have enlisted respected scholars and practitioners in their camps, and all three have their proponents. Not surprisingly, all three are well represented on the Internet, where their popular websites continue to enlist new adherents.

To date, at least in the medical community of the United States, the brain dysfunction idea remains the most widely accepted. However, some of its strongest adherents have been criticized for potential conflicts of interest. (CHADD, for example, receives significant financial support from the makers of Ritalin, and has been named as a codefendant in a class-action suit brought by parents who feel their children have suffered ill effects from Ritalin.[15]) Most teachers favor the medical view as well, especially when they are at their wit's end dealing with children who just don't seem to listen.

Ultimately the decision about medication is the parent's to make. As the researchers involved in an exhaustive longitudinal study of ADHD (funded by the National Institute of Mental Health and the Department of Education) point out, current research results "highlight the need for caution and argue against a 'one size fits all' approach to treatment."[16] In other words, there is no clear consensus about this diagnosis or how to treat it. Parents will have to review the pros and cons, and make up their own minds.

## Our Position

This book takes a neutral position on the controversy itself, in an effort to stay focused on the needs of individual parents. Keep in mind that you do not have to decide the controversy in general terms; your task is only to decide *what is best for your individual child*. In my years of practice as a child and family therapist, I have seen numerous youngsters diagnosed and medicated when, I thought, other measures would have been more appropriate and useful. Julie, the author of our "Teacher Tips," has a less jaundiced view. She believes most of the children she has taught who were on medication were helped by it, at least helped to function in a school setting. Several of the graduate students I have taught over the years were diagnosed with ADHD as adults, and without exception they found the diagnosis a boon, an explanation for their previous academic problems—and a chance to improve. I don't want to invalidate their experience, since a growing number of adults are now claiming the ADHD diagnosis for themselves. Yet I am troubled by the exponential increase in the use of Ritalin in the

## From a Former Inattentive Child

Zach is twenty-five years old now. He and a friend run a highly successful, lucrative business designing Web pages for certain types of businesses. He is finishing his undergraduate degree in computer science, mostly through courses taken on-line. His parents are both professionals, and his older brother is a medical student now entering his residency. For much of his life, Zach has been (to use his own phrase) "the failing one." His success is still new and precious to him.

"You asked me, 'Zach, did you dislike school as a child?' I didn't 'dislike' school. I *hated* school, hated it with a passion. From the beginning, it felt to me like a record they were playing at the wrong speed. Everything in school just always went so slow. The teachers would talk, *yada yada yada*, on and on, and the other kids would be whispering and scraping their chairs, and there would be, like, this buzzing in my head sort of. I couldn't wait to get out of there. Every day I would be the first one out of the school building. At home I would play Nintendo for hours—I was like the video-game king; all the kids called me that. It helped a little, being good at the games, because I sure wasn't good at anything in school.

"Things got a little bit better when my dad got me the computer. I could fool around with that some, and after a while everyone, even my older brother, the brain, came to me when their computers needed fixing. But still, I never thought of that as, like, a skill. That was just what I was doing when I was supposed to be doing my homework. And I knew everybody (but my dad), the teachers and people, they just thought I was dumb.

"I made mostly C's in high school, some D's, but I scraped into some kind of a college. In college this guy in my dorm sold me some Ritalin. I had never been diagnosed as ADHD—my parents took me to a psychologist, and he just said I had average I.Q. And my pediatrician, he didn't know. But I knew I had all the symptoms. And that Ritalin was wild. When I took that pill, I could actually sit down and read a book all in one sitting. It sped everything up around me. But, I don't know, it was like I wasn't myself. This college doctor I went to said I had ADHD for sure, and that he would prescribe me the stuff, but I thought about it, and I said no.

"Then my friend, he was like, 'My dad has this business, and he needs a Web page, and they don't know how,' and I was like, 'I can do that,' and one thing led to another. Now I can start work when I want to, at midnight if I want to. I can work as fast as I want. And I get paid for it! Someday soon, I'm going back to my old middle school. I'm going to call on the vice-principal there, the one who always said I would end up flipping burgers. I'll be driving my Lexus, wearing my Armani. And I'll stroll right in, say to him, 'Hey there, Mr. Smith! It's our world now, the people like me, and your model is obsolete.'"

United States and what that may imply about our country. In short, this issue is complicated, and it would be presumptuous to try to make this decision for you.

What we do want to do is stress *your right as a parent* to make an informed decision. Therefore, we are presenting all sides of this issue, with an emphasis on factors to consider as you make your judgment. Based on our common experience, and my best clinical judgment, we do want to establish some basic parameters or guidelines for that decision. We recommend that you choose not to administer psychostimulant medication to a child under the age of six, that you explore other options before deciding to medicate, and that you choose a treatment plan for your child that, even if it includes medication, is not limited to medication.

The first recommendation should be clear. Current medical opinion, including the *Physician's Desk Reference*, is against prescribing psychostimulants to children under six. In our opinion, this is an excellent caution, given both the wide developmental variability in this age group and the ample opportunity for greater maturation to take care of the problem. But, sadly, prescriptions for children in this age group are increasing in number, despite the warnings, as some physicians yield to pressure from teachers and parents.

"Don't worry, she'll grow out of it" was one piece of advice Janet received. As Ashley is already in the third grade, Janet may be excused for feeling a greater sense of urgency, since Ashley may indeed be falling too far behind academically to catch up. And as the growing number of adults who feel they have ADHD attest, some individuals apparently never "grow out of" their difficulties. However, if Ashley were four years old, this would be excellent advice. The naturally short attention span of a preschooler is not to be confused with anything medically abnormal. Moreover, what is learned in the preschool years, while vitally important, has to do with getting along with other people, loving oneself and others, and so on. Any little deficiencies in such academic areas as memorizing the alphabet can easily be made up in first grade. Therefore, if you are being pressured to find a doctor who will prescribe medication for your restless child of three or four years, our advice is to find another, more progressive preschool instead.

In addition, in our opinion, medication should not be considered either as a first or as a sole treatment for attention deficit disorder—at any age. If you do decide to give your child medication, it will be far more effective if it is backed up with appropriate changes at home and at school. And if you prefer not to medicate your child, these same changes in many cases suffice to bring about improvements in the desired areas. NIMH– and Department of Education–funded researchers, all psychiatrists committed to pharmaceutical treatment, nonetheless found that 75 percent of children given only behavioral treatment did fine without the medication, and that their parents were actually more satisfied with the results than were the parents of the children who had been given medication.[17] Ritalin, Dexedrine, and Adderall are potentially dangerous psychostimulants, listed with the Drug Enforcement Administration as controlled substances. Administering any of them to your growing child, therefore, surely calls for thoughtful consideration. It is never the only option, nor is it the place to start, when you begin trying to help your child with his or her attentional problems.

A little applied common sense can't hurt, may help a great deal, and is completely free of side effects. So let's start there. We'll delineate specific steps you can try at home, whether your child is having major or only minor problems attending and concentrating. In the process, we'll revisit more of Janet's advisors and clarify more partial truths. We will then describe modifications that can be made in the school setting, should these other earlier steps prove insufficient, as well as the option of placing the child in a different type of school. For more extreme situations (that is, when these changes have proved ineffective) we will then revisit the medication question and discuss other equally forceful alternatives as well.

# Commonsense Basics of Helping Your Child

The place to start is back at the beginning, with a careful examination of your child. Look carefully at your home context as well.

## Start at the Doctor's Office

While it is true that a child already on medication may benefit from the more sophisticated medication management of a specialist (as Janet's school psychologist implied, "Your child should be seeing a child psychiatrist"), the child psychiatrist is also correct that this medical branch is not the first step ("Her family doctor is most qualified to make the initial diagnosis"). The first step is to rule out any sort of physical condition that can make it difficult for the child to attend in school and keep up with class work. Any type of illness, for example, can make a child distracted. Adults who feel weak and ill generally become less active, even noticeably drowsy. But children have so much more natural energy than adults do that they often react to fatigue and discomfort with increased agitation.

Think back to when your child was two or three years old and stayed up too late or got too excited at bedtime. Anyone who has ever had to put an overtired toddler to bed knows that up until the point when the child is actually asleep, he will show his weariness by running around in circles, giggling, and generally acting like a windup toy unable to stop itself. In just the same way, a school-age child who is run down will often act wound up. In particular, the child should be tested for thyroid abnormalities and for common food allergies, two conditions the National Institutes of Health has found may be confused with ADHD.[18] Sleep disorders should be ruled out as well.

## Do Health Checkups at Home

Difficulties in paying attention seem to have some link to diet. It is not true that sweets alone explain inattentiveness ("Look at how hyper the kids are after Halloween"), although parents and teachers do complain about their charges the day after holidays. However, in some cases a balanced diet and a good daily multivitamin can improve behaviors in kids thought to be exhibiting ADHD. In other cases, essential fatty acids (EFA) have been helpful. If your pediatrician concurs, an EFA supplement may be useful.[19]

Evaluate also whether your child needs more sleep and is getting plenty of physical exercise. Schools today are cutting down on recess and outside playtime, in favor of increased academics; after-school day-care programs may also focus on homework, crafts activities, and less active, indoor play. Many children in urban areas are not allowed to play outdoors unsupervised; and inside there is always the lure of TV, radio, and computer. All too often this adds up to a daily schedule almost devoid of unrestrained physical play.

The lessening of vigorous activity explains why more American children than ever are overweight. It may also explain why some youngsters are having trouble paying attention in school. Children need the outlet for tension that exercise provides, and should be encouraged to run, jump, and tumble flat out for at least an hour or two a day. Without this, they may be fidgety in school and find it difficult to sleep at night. It is far preferable for them to burn energy in free play outside, and then sleep soundly, than to spend their day in a nervous half state, not really physically active but not really resting either. Don't assume that because your child is involved in sports, exercise is not an issue. Coaches focused on winning games often spend time on fatiguing drills, which, while they may improve performance, don't relieve tension the way unstructured free play does. Soccer practice is no substitute for splashing in mud puddles.

## Watch for "Invisible" Stimulants Your Child May Consume

Stimulants can produce a rebound effect, in which the child is more inattentive than ever and possibly restless and twitchy as well. You are probably not giving your child obvious stimulants, such as strong coffee, diet pills, and over-the-counter "alertness aids." (If you are, stop!) But many carbonated soft drinks, often marketed to children, have as much or more caffeine than coffee. (Read the label.) In addition, some over-the-counter and prescription medications may make it difficult for children to concentrate. Allergy medications are common culprits, producing either agitated behavior or extreme drowsiness or both.

Check to see what your children are consuming mentally as well. In twenty years of practice, I have yet to see a child diagnosed with ADHD who didn't spend at least two hours a day playing animated video games. I am not suggesting a direct causal link; often it's impossible to tell if the symptoms came about before or after the intense interest in video games, and it may well be, as the Indigo people suggest, that this type of child is simply drawn to this type of play. But it does make sense that a child's getting used to making quick movements requiring eye-hand coordination without speech being involved, while watching rapid, repetitive, unceasing action, may not be the best preparation for attending to the voice of a real live, *comparatively motionless* human being. If you have trouble rousing your child from his absorption in video games to come to supper, it is likely his teacher is also having some trouble gaining his attention. If you do not already have a video-game console set up in your home, consider putting your money into a home computer instead. Even if you do have such a setup, see if you can wean your child gradually to playing computer games. From these (preferably nonviolent, but still exciting) computer games, it is only a step to educational software, and from there to computer programming and other potentially useful life skills. Skills exclusively related to blowing up alien spaceships on your TV screen are less in demand.

Notice what TV shows and movies your children watch. A steady diet of bloodthirsty vampires and sexually charged music videos is disturbing to preteens and even to teens (and, of course, even more disturbing to younger children, who might be better watching "Barney"). No matter how "cool" youths insist they are, it is likely they retain anxiety-producing images in their minds, which can interrupt their sleep and may distract them the next day. Try substituting an old movie the family can watch together, a night of family board games, a walk around the block, or a parent-child project, such as baking a cake together. Much as they will deny it, children have nerves, too, and sometimes they overstimulate themselves to the point of nervous exhaustion, unless they are steered into more soothing, wholesome activities.

## Recheck Relationships and Routines

Ellen's advice to Janet was needlessly guilt-producing and overly focused on one event (the promotion). But it contained what may be a core of truth—"Your child needs more attention from you." Sometimes the deficit children suffer is actually in their parents' attention. This can happen even in conscientious, loving families, simply because everyone is so busy. All children need daily, intense attention from their parent(s), and some children seem as well to need a great deal of parental structure. Here are a few questions to consider.

## Do You Have a Smoothly Flowing Daily Routine?

If you are always running late and out of breath, your child may be a bit flustered as well. In today's busy world, with both parents working outside the home and children also involved in outside activities, the chaos of getting everyone off to school and work can be like waking up into a bad dream. You might regard your child's attention problems as an opportunity to revisit the morning nightmare. It may be worthwhile to wake up a half hour earlier to start the day less frenetically. Review Julie's paper-chasing tips from Chapter 2, giving special attention to the nightly ritual of backpack unpacking (without which my own child would never get to school in one piece and without tears). Enlist your spouse and older children in the effort, and see if you can collectively come up with some good ideas to streamline household routines.

## Are You Letting Go of What You Can?

If you are gulping coffee all day long just to make it through your schedule, it may be no wonder that your child seems to need stimulants as well. If something has to go, remember that what is most important for your children is your steady presence. From a child's perspective, it's better to eat take-out pizza with a cheerful father who is then ready to help with homework than it is to have a father who cooks five-course gourmet meals but gets exhausted and cross. As my then ten-year-old daughter once said to me when I had been very busy at work and was relieving my guilt by frantically whipping up a batch of homemade cookies, "Don't bake for me, Mama; just be with me."

The dust on the furniture will wait; if there is limited time, spend it relaxing with your children.

## Are You Allowing Your Child Time to Be a Child?

Sometimes it is the child's schedule that is the culprit. School-age children can rarely handle more than one scheduled after-school activity a week, whether it's piano lessons, a soccer team, or an art class. Even this one activity should be led by a teacher or coach who has reasonable expectations, not one who expects a consuming amount of practice. Encourage your child's strongest interest, and avoid trying to keep up with the child down the street who has lessons every day of the week. If your child wants to be involved with more activities, explain that you will start by supporting and encouraging (and transporting to) one activity per school semester. If the child can handle this one activity while keeping his grades up, and doesn't show any signs of exhaustion or distraction, then you can consider a second. But keep reviewing the schedule—if you feel as if you're living behind the wheel of your car, transporting here and there, then something is out of balance.

## Do You Have a Crisp, Authoritative Style of Discipline?

Many busy working parents fall into a discipline style that can best be described as "talky." A typical scenario may go something like this: Susan just got off work an hour ago, but there is no rest for the single parent, and she has already picked up her children at day care and made a trip to the grocery store. Now Susan is trying to unpack the groceries, start supper, keep the cat out of the tuna-fish casserole she is starting to prepare, and talk to her five-year-old, Sally, all at the same time. Meanwhile, her older child, Johnny, is entertaining himself by bending his radio's antenna back and forth. "Stop that, Johnny," Mom calls, "I mean it! Stop it right now; that will break. And anyway you listen to way too much of that rap music. And another thing. . . . What is it, Sally? Your teacher said what? Fluffy, get off the counter!" Johnny continues his experiments, secure in the knowledge that it will be several more minutes before Mom actually comes out of the kitchen to stop him.

There is nothing hugely wrong with such a discipline style. This talky style is a fit with the middle-class American "dialect" that teachers also use. As long as Mom comes out of the kitchen and takes action eventually, Johnny will get the appropriate message. Unfortunately, though, Johnny is also getting a message that won't work so well in a school setting. Johnny is learning to tune out the first ten minutes of most adult-child interactions. In a school setting, in a classroom of perhaps thirty-five or more students, Johnny's teacher cannot afford the luxury of waiting. She may talk for a while, too, but if Johnny ignores her while she is talking, he will be seen as uncooperative or inattentive or both. In school, Johnny won't get ten minutes to keep playing. Some children can handle this difference in context; others don't make the adjustment as well.

If you typically talk a while before your child actually listens, and your child's teacher is describing him as inattentive, it may be helpful to moderate your discipline style at home. If you think you don't talk that much, if your impression is that you say "Jump!" and your children jump, or if you are like most of us busy working parents, it may be helpful—if painful—to leave a tape recorder running during the busiest times of day at your house. Hear for yourself how often you become background noise. A helpful source for those wishing to adopt a somewhat brisker discipline style is *1-2-3 Magic*.[20]

OK, so you have considered all of the above questions and steps. Your child is physically quite healthy, and your home environment is as structured and calm as it seems likely to get.

But your child's teacher still complains that he or she is not paying attention, not concentrating, or not on task. The next step is to consider making modifications in the school routine.

## What Can Change at School

When considering changes at your child's school, the most useful thing you can do is to begin to pinpoint exactly *in what ways* your child is inattentive. The ADHD diagnosis lumps together many behaviors: being distracted, daydreaming, acting out impulsively, being physically aggressive, exhibiting abundant energy, and fidgeting restlessly. It will be helpful if you can identify the problem areas more precisely, and the following questions may assist you in doing that.

### *Is Your Child Primarily Active, Restless, Talkative, and Impulsive?*

Notice whether your child's primary behaviors include being very active physically. Is he up out of his seat frequently? Does he complain that school is "boring" or "repetitive"? Are there more behavioral than academic problems? These actions can equally describe a female child. They describe a child who is more hyperactive than inattentive. Here are some modifications to consider for the school program.

**Allowing More Physical Exercise**
One child whom I worked with benefited greatly from the school principal's decision to let him eat his lunch outdoors, in the company of the gym coach, and run a few laps before returning to class. This required a cooperative principal and

coach, but it didn't cost any extra money or time, and it allowed the child to focus much better on his afternoon work, having discharged some nervous energy. Running a mile or two concentrates the mind wonderfully for some children. Consider ways that your child might get to include more physical exercise at school.

## Participating in a Gifted-Talented Program

Is the child eligible to be in a program for gifted or talented youngsters? If not, will the regular classroom teacher consider adding extra enrichment or creative activities for your child to do? Your child may simply be bored. If this is the case, having the child take an intelligence test administered by a qualified psychologist is the first step toward placement in a more challenging academic program. Clues to ADHD sometimes show up in intelligence testing as a scattered pattern of uneven results, but the diagnosis must still be confirmed by a physician. Giftedness, however, can be confirmed (for school-placement purposes) by a psychologist using results from an intelligence test. So be sure to make it clear to the psychologist that it is the giftedness you most want to explore through this testing. If your child happens to test out as both gifted *and* having ADHD, deal with the giftedness first. (Review Chapter 4 on the accelerated child for how to do this.) Your child may settle down greatly once he or she is not so bored. If the child has poor behavior but acceptable grades (at least on tests and non-routine activities), it is worth trying an enrichment program even if the intelligence test results don't show giftedness; inattentiveness can artificially depress the results of intelligence tests, and the child may be bored with everything—*including* the test.

### An Alternative School Might Help

Like Gwendolyn, the child cited by the third of Janet's parent advisors, some children diagnosed with ADHD do very well in a private school of the alternative type (see Chapter 1 for a review of types of schools). Consider whether your child might benefit from an alternative school. A Waldorf-type format, for example, which allows for self-pacing, increased physical activity, and more varied tasks, may be just the change that is needed. To test out this idea, try your child in a summer camp or after-school program run by the alternative school before you commit to the school-year's program.

### Consider Home Schooling

Even if you do not conduct full-time home schooling, could extra tutoring at home be beneficial? Some very active children may benefit from computer-based, on-line education.[21] With such a format, the child can get up, run around, and even play basketball between learning sessions. There are no peers to distract him or for him to bother. And some restless children seem to have a natural affinity for the computer, especially for video game–like experiences. This home tutoring also helps children who wake up late in the day, as many restless children seem to do.

## Is Your Child Quiet and Withdrawn?

Is your daughter slow to adapt to change around her? Does she complain that her school is too noisy, too crowded, or too "busy"? Is she easily distracted, nervously flitting from one activity to another? Are her difficulties more academic than behavioral? (These reactions could equally characterize a son.) These behaviors describe a child who is more inattentive than hyperactive. Here are some modifications to consider for the school program.

## Ask What Those Daydreams Are About

Sometimes intensely creative children escape into a world of their own, especially if they feel threatened by the world outside. Have a calm, nonjudgmental conversation with your son or daughter about his or her thoughts and feelings. This is also a chance to check for any sad or worried thoughts that could be preoccupying your child. Provide a permitted outlet, such as a journal, in which your child can record thoughts. The classroom teacher may be able to allow time for this activity in class, once other work is done. The earlier suggestions for testing for the gifted program, given for the more active child, apply equally to this more inwardly turned child.

## Find a Quieter, More Structured School

Some quiet, more withdrawn children (like Reginald, mentioned by the second of Janet's parent advisors) may do well in a smaller class that has more structure. Such a situation can often be found in the religious type of private school. Alternative schools may also be an option, if the atmosphere is quiet and orderly. An alternative school is most likely to be a good fit when the child has strong artistic or other creative talents, and the school promotes these forms of expression. Again, try before you buy—sign up for a summer camp or after-school program first, before committing to a complete school year. In the public-school classroom, you might ask for an older child to act as a tutor for part of the day, and look for a classroom teacher who is especially skilled at creating a gentle, calm environment. Being in a smaller class may be helpful as well to your youngster.

### Try Some Home Schooling

Would home tutoring help with the academic problems? A quiet child is less likely to benefit from the razzle-dazzle of technology, and more likely to need guidance from a nearby human being. A patient parent, or a full-time tutor, can provide one-on-one attention and help with focusing. At home the child is also free from the distraction of peers and the hustle and bustle of changing classes, making her way through the halls, and so on. Indeed, attention difficulties with more withdrawn youngsters are particularly likely to show up when they are overwhelmed by the transition from elementary to middle school. Try out the home schooling with a little tutoring or one course before committing to anything full-time. And, again, online curriculums are available that considerably reduce the parent's load in home schooling.

When requesting any modifications from your public school, keep in mind that your child is eligible under IDEA for any special treatment he or she may require if there has been a diagnosis of attention deficit disorder. Your observations and the teacher's observations are likely to be key determinants, and the school psychologist's testing may be helpful as well, but these are not enough to satisfy federal regulations. For your child to be eligible for exceptional student education, and, hence, to push for any changes your child's teacher is not initially willing to make, a diagnosis of ADHD must be confirmed by a physician.

# What If It's Still Not Working?

When you have made changes both at home and at school, but you and your child are still frustrated, you may wish to consider medication. To have this option, a diagnosis of ADHD must

## Family Activity

Since books and websites in this category are so polemic or politicized, I tried to compensate by offering you not one, but two, relaxing family activities to do as you make your way through the maze of conflicting opinions and decide what is best for *your* child.

For the first, try logging on to www.keirsey.com. Have everyone take the on-line personality quizzes, based on Jungian psychology. Can you see how someone with an Artisan personality type could have trouble in school? Did your temperament type fit you, resonating with your sense of self? How well would your type do in a conventional school environment? While this site takes a very clear position, advocating alternative schooling instead of medication, you don't have to agree with that to enjoy the idea of focusing on one's strengths and accepting individual differences.

Second, try some advanced computer fun. Log onto http://angelfire.lycos.com, play some games, and build yourself a free family home page. Be sure your child gets a chance to be the leader in this process.

have been made by a physician who is also willing to prescribe stimulant medication. If you do decide to try it, here are some useful guidelines, based on my experience working with parents who have utilized the medication option.

• **Don't stop commonsense options.** Psychostimulant medication is not magic, and it will not automatically compensate for disorganization at home or a poor fit between your child and the school. Keep trying what you had been using—the medicine is an added treatment, not a replacement for other helps.

- **Watch carefully for the medication's side effects.** Be sure to inform the prescribing physician of any side effects you notice your child showing from ingesting the medication. Besides the failure to gain weight and height, already mentioned, other side effects that psychostimulants are known to sometimes cause include depression, sleeplessness or sleep disturbance, twitching, and, especially in teenagers, the development of vocal tics (throat clearing, sniffing, excessive coughing) or motor tics (blinking, facial grimacing, and spasmodic shrugging or head turning). Your physician cannot know these things are happening unless he or she is kept informed. Let the doctor decide what is "important enough to mention," rather than waiting to share the information until it has perhaps become a larger problem.

- **Don't involve the school in medication issues.** With the best intentions in the world, sometimes teachers and school officials fall into a pattern of being "junior physicians" about these medication issues. For example, your child's teacher may ask if your child's dose has been lowered (or raised), "because I notice he was a little worse (or better) today." Children do vary from day to day in their behavior or reactions, and it is generally not useful to allow school personnel to relate too much to your child's medication. If you can possibly avoid having the child given medication at school, do so. Even if you cannot, answer comments about the medication with something noncommittal, like "We leave all that to Doctor X, but I will certainly pass on your observations."

By the way, if your son or daughter is diagnosed with ADHD, but you decide *not* to give your child psychostimulant medication, my advice would be exactly the same. If someone at the school asks, simply say that you have discussed the situation with the child's doctor, a decision regarding the appropriate level of medication has been reached (which in your case may be a level of zero, but that is between you and the physician you have chosen), and now you would like to turn the conversation back to educational issues. Getting into a debate with your child's teacher about the pros and cons of medication is both a waste of time and an invitation to keep reopening the issue. Teachers and school officials who take a great interest in a child's medication are just trying to be helpful. Nevertheless, such a focus by school personnel can confirm the child's view of himself as a "sick" individual, involve you in micromanaging the dose, take away from your authority as the one person with the right to decide what medication your child takes, annoy your doctor, and distract the teacher from getting to know your child as a whole person. Smile pleasantly and change the subject.

• **Evaluate and reevaluate.** Check on a regular basis to see if the medication seems to be helping. Have clear objectives about what changes you hope to see. If something doesn't feel right to you, get a second opinion.

• **Talk with your child about selling medicine.** Sooner or later (yes, even in a "nice" suburban school district), your child will be approached by another child wishing to buy his prescription medicine. Explain to your child that this is illegal and dangerous. Again, it helps if the child can avoid taking a dose of medicine at school. Keep open the lines of communication, especially as your child gets older, so he can discuss his thoughts and feelings about both medication and illegal drugs.

## Alternatives to Medication

Perhaps you think that your child has a serious problem, yet are not comfortable with psychostimulant medications. Several other avenues of treatment are available that are also related in various degrees to physiology. Here are some alternatives you might wish to explore.

- **Martial arts and other Eastern exercise programs.** Some parents of children diagnosed with ADHD attest to the calm and poise they have seen their children develop through training in a martial art. If karate seems too aggressive to you, tai chi is a good alternative. So is yoga, with its emphasis on calming the body.
- **Biofeedback.** Children (and adults) can be trained to monitor their own autonomic responses. Eventually, they become able to slow down breathing and even the heart rate. This is a well-researched option for children (and adults) who tend to become too agitated, and the results are usually quite positive.[22] To find a qualified biofeedback practitioner, ask your family doctor, your dentist, or your state's medical society.
- **Interactive metronome training.** A new treatment modality that has been developed in recent years, developing interactive work with a metronome is a commercial operation—and not a cheap one. But the initial research results have been promising. The program teaches children to tap in time with a steadily ticking metronome, which is then set for more and more difficult sequences as the training continues. The thinking is that the child learns to attend very precisely, and that this training in attentiveness generalizes to other situations.[23]

## The Big Picture

Above all, keep your eye on life *after* school. Whatever the merits of the diagnosis, no one disagrees that individuals with ADHD–type symptoms can and do lead productive adult lives. Prominent individuals who seem to have fit the diagnostic criteria for ADHD as children include such notables as Leonardo da Vinci, Pablo Picasso, and Thomas Edison. Much research has demonstrated a link between traits associated with ADHD and traits associated with creativity. Whatever your child makes of his life as an adult, nothing will ever be as hard for him again as fitting in with a standardized school system. Remind him, and yourself, that options expand as you grow up.

School is a preparation for life, but it is not life, and, if you can just get your child through enough schooling to suffice, life in the real world is going to be a vast improvement. Adulthood beckons; don't lose sight of the delightful aspects of your child's energetic, creative, and fanciful qualities along the way. One day you both will be glad of them.

## TEACHER TIPS

These are some tips that may help you and your child work with teachers to compensate for or overcome problems with staying on task.

### Some Children Just Aren't Made for Sitting Behind a Desk

If you can investigate alternative schooling, great. If you find that it will take medication to keep your child in school, my suggestion is to find a competent physician and get the prescription. But do remind the child that this is a temporary accommodation to an environment that is not very flexible, not a commentary on him or her as a person. The world needs warriors, explorers, and inventors, too—we just can't always fit them comfortably into the classroom environment.

### Sometimes Children Need More Order in Their Chaotic Lives

For every truly "different" child, I see two or three who just have a few more transitions than they can handle in their lives. At times I believe the ADHD diagnosis does reflect a truly different way of being in the world. But more often I have seen it used for children who could benefit from more organization and structure at home. Life can be chaotic, struggling with blended families, single-parent families, dual-career couples, or all the other innovations of the early twenty-first century. But some things do not change, and one of them is that children need an orderly, predictable home life in order to do well in school. If your child is bounced back and forth between two (or more) houses during the week or has no predictable homework, bath, or bedtime, that is not a neurological problem. Children enjoy repetitive routines, ones that can seem boring and limited to an adult. Adults may need to set aside some of their own gratification, temporarily, to provide a stable nest during the school years. This is true even if your kid really *is* different and creative.

### Be Extra Nice to Your Child's Teacher

Your child is not an easy one to teach, especially in a standardized, structured setting. Try to praise what you can in the efforts made by your child's teacher. Make a special effort yourself: volunteer to help out during field trips, special events, and classroom parties, situations in which your impulsive child may not be at his best. Consider using on-line instruction and hiring a tutor, for occasional breaks and supplements, even if not for the long haul. And by all means give your child access to a computer. These days, you can find access to computers at almost all public libraries and even at many shopping malls. If ever a child needed to be connected to the World Wide Web, it is this child we are discussing. He's wired anyway; let him be wired constructively.

**Look for the Positives About Your Child, and Enjoy Them**
So maybe your child is never going to win a good-conduct prize or get straight A's. I bet, though, he is fun and lively to be around, and full of creative ideas. Enjoy your child for who he is. Who knows? You may be raising the next Thomas Edison! Or, at least the next Bill Gates (who, by the way, dropped out of college and attended a special alternative high school . . . makes you wonder).

# Resources

Sadly, parents of children with attention difficulties cannot turn to the same kind of warm, open-minded, on-line community that parents of accelerated children or children with other learning differences have. The ADHD area has become so politicized that most of the websites are shrill in tone, and relentless in pushing one particular viewpoint. For the most part, dissent is not well tolerated.

The endnotes for this topic, on the other hand, are the most extensive among the chapters of this book. As with dealing with the phonics controversy in Chapter 5, I have tried to provide a maximum amount of access to original research in controversial areas, so that you, as a parent, can make up your own mind. If you form strong convictions on one or the other side of the controversy, the more politicized websites (listed in the endnotes) will embrace you. If not, you may wish to try Dr. Lawrence Diller's website, docdiller.com, the only one I could find where multiple viewpoints are entertained. It was at his website that I found the magic words, "Parents don't need to feel guilty whatever they decide."

# 7

# "Nobody Likes Me!"

## The Unhappy Child

Maggie and Caitlin are best friends. That is, they were best friends until yesterday. When eight-year-old Maggie went skipping over to play with her during recess yesterday, Caitlin said that she is now Jennifer's best friend instead. Caitlin and Jennifer have formed a club, the main rule of which is that Maggie cannot be a member. All during recess, Maggie stood and watched as the other two girls played happily at being a club. She tried to protest a few times, but was told, "Jennifer started this club, and only popular girls can be in it."

This morning at breakfast, Maggie asked her mother if she can change schools. "Nonsense, dear," her mother responded. "This is the school we selected for you, and anyway you would miss your sweet little friend Caitlin." Maggie mashed up her corn flakes and cheered herself up by imagining that Caitlin was at the bottom of the sea or was being eaten by sharks.

Mr. Green is a very popular teacher; all the middle school students agree about that. The other teachers respect him because he is so good at keeping order in his classroom, and he has such a great sense of humor, too.

The only trouble is, right now Frank doesn't think Mr. Green is funny. Frank has a big crush on Angela. He wrote her a note during Mr. Green's lecture ("Deer Angela: I think your hot. Frank Smith"), but when he was trying to pass it to Angela, Mr. Green saw what he was doing and intercepted the note. Now Mr. Green is reading the note out loud, asking sarcastically, "Is this what passes for romantic poetry these days? Or does our young swain just not know any words of more than one syllable? I notice spelling is a difficulty. . . ."

Everyone is laughing, even Angela. Everyone is laughing except Frank, that is. Frank's face is red and he is thinking about how far he could get if he ran away from home to avoid ever having to go back to school.

Emily makes one excuse after another to get out of going to high school. One day her stomach hurts; the next, she has a toothache, or she feels a cold coming on; and so on. Emily's mother, Rose, is so busy and distracted these days that she doesn't really notice how many days of school Emily is missing. After all, Rose is going through a bitter divorce while trying to start a new job and adjust to living in a cramped apartment alone with Emily. Rose knows her daughter is having some adjustment difficulties, too, but she figures time will sort these out. She hasn't talked to Emily about the divorce because it is complicated and she really doesn't know what to say. Meanwhile, in the absence of an explanation from her mother or father, Emily has decided that it must be Rose's new boyfriend, Dan, who is causing the divorce and that if Dan were not in the picture, everything would be just like it used to be. So Emily wants to be home in case Dan shows up. If and when he does, Emily plans to chase him away. The last time Emily did make it to school, she startled her friends by asking if anyone knew where she could buy a gun.

Maggie, Frank, and Emily are unhappy, too unhappy to concentrate on their schoolwork. While Maggie's problems may seem trivial compared to Emily's, that is only because for most of us it has been a long time since we felt the sting of typical third-grade cruelty. Looking back through the glasses of memory, we may see childhood as a gentle and peaceful time. But the everyday reality of childhood for those still living it is that it hurts—often. Even the most privileged children have to learn the sad basic lessons that you can't trust everyone, everyone does not love you, and life is not always fair.

Not every child struggles with a learning disability. Nor is every child habitually restless or bored in school. But every child is unhappy at times, and that is what makes sorting out these complaints especially tricky. No parent wants to ignore the signs of serious trouble, but wise parents also know that they cannot protect their children from every emotional bump and scrape. The challenge lies in determining when to intervene to protect your son or daughter from cruel peers, sadistic teachers, or family problems that are getting out of hand, while not overreacting to unhappy experiences that are simply a natural part of the child's growing up process.

In previous chapters we have assumed that a given child's academic struggles are causing unhappiness with school, but, of course, the opposite can be true as well. Acute unhappiness makes it virtually impossible to concentrate on learning, and can therefore cause academic problems. Even when a learning difference is a major part of the problem, while that difficulty is being resolved it is important to keep an eye on the child's overall level of unhappiness. Simply by virtue of being children, youngsters lack impulse control and good judgment, and seriously unhappy children do foolish and desperate things.

In this chapter we discuss strategies for preventing everyday problems from escalating, helping when a child needs guidance, and intervening when the situation becomes critical. The strategies involve establishing some basic guidelines for what constitutes everyday difficulties, how to tell when a child needs help and counseling or advice, and how to tell when it is time to intervene forcefully. The interpersonal context of school— the child's relationships with peers and teachers—is stressful for all children at times, and can become toxic for some, in certain circumstances. And although this book is oriented to school problems, we would be remiss not to consider the possibility that family issues are affecting your child more than you may realize, and that the primary issue might be home rather than school. So we will consider prevention, help, and intervention with respect to problems with peers, problems with teachers, and problems at home.

The other chapters in this part included excerpts from interviews with adults who had struggled as children with the learning differences being discussed. But every adult reading this book, unless you were almost unbelievably sheltered as a child, will have had experience with teasing peers, with at least a mildly unfair teacher or two, and with family quarrels. So in lieu of the interview, each section will include empathy exercises, to help you think yourself back into the kinds of situations your child may be facing now.

## What's Normal in Relating to Peers?

Starting from about the age of six, children begin to think in the same categories as the adults who have raised them. So, if youngsters have been raised in a society that categorizes certain people as physically unattractive or socially undesirable, they will make those judgments about other children. Particularly in the elementary school years, their judgments tend to be harsher than adults', since they do not yet have much grasp of the com-

## Problems with Peers

Try this exercise to help you remember what teasing is like for a child. Pick out something to wear that is not considered appropriate for your age and gender. This will probably vary, depending on where in the country you live. If you're a woman, in most places the exercise will work if you scrub your face clean of makeup, cover your hair completely with a man's hat (shaving your head would work even better, but there likely are limits to your willingness to experiment), and wear men's shoes. If you're a man, you might wear lipstick along with at least one article of pink clothing. Once dressed in this manner, go someplace where you will be surrounded by many people of your own age group whom you did not select, people you don't know well. (You might visit a large regional mall to encounter this population.) Notice how uncomfortable you feel, how long you can last before you feel a need to begin providing explanations to strangers ("I'm just doing this because I was reading this book . . ."), and what kind of questions and comments are addressed to you. (Women typically begin to feel invisible as salespeople and others ignore them; men are more likely to be harassed and may even be questioned by the security guard in some locales. Be careful; discontinue the experiment if you're getting hostile vibes.) Ask yourself, How much harder would this be if I were a child, still unsure of my ability to conform? Even as an adult, how much am I constrained by what others might think of me?

plexity of life. An adult seeing a child with a limp, for example, knows to consider that this may be an injury, the result of illness, a temporary sprain, a birth defect, or a hereditary condition, among other possibilities. In contrast, ask a typical eight-year-old child, and you will get a simplistic explanation, such as "Probably that kid limps because he was kicking when he wasn't supposed to and so he broke something about his foot. That won't happen to me because I'm good." Children tend to habitually blame the victim to a degree we hope adults outgrow. And children tend to see any kind of noticeable difference—wearing glasses, having an oddly shaped head, being behind or ahead of the rest of the class academically, even having a funny name—as valid grounds for these rigid judgments.

Little girls are especially at risk from each other. As my colleague Margo Weiss perceptively remarks, "Little boys play war; little girls have wars." Contrary as these words may be to our pink, sugar image of little girls, they make a good point. Having comparatively advanced verbal and cognitive development in the elementary school years *and* still displaying a greater physical timidity than boys, most girls tend to express their natural competitiveness through an almost endless round of verbal skirmishes. Your eight- or nine-year-old son may scuffle physically with his friends, but the worst that is likely to happen to him in the process is a bruise or two. Your daughter of the same age may come home looking tidy, but inwardly seething because of the latest round of social warfare in her peer group. Who is more "popular" (popular here should really be translated as "powerful," rather than anything resembling pleasant and likeable)? Who's in and who's out of the "clubs" that little girls endlessly form and reform? Above all, who has stolen someone else's "best friend"? These remain common preoccupations of elementary-school-age girls.

In middle school, the two genders begin to spend more time interacting with each other, to their overall mutual benefit. Boys typically become less rough and gradually less likely to think burping is invariably hilarious; girls typically begin to emerge a bit from their intense relationships with each other. But this process takes time, and in its early stages, it unfortunately produces one specific area of increased, rather than reduced, harshness. Middle school children are so anxious about their emerging sexuality, and so confused about the guidelines from adult society (What exactly *is* a manly man or a womanly woman these days, anyway? And how do you go about learning to be one?), that they react with great severity when peers seem to them to have their gender roles wrong. A girl who is perceived as unattractive or unfeminine in middle school will suffer. And the hapless boy who is perceived as effeminate is likely to wish he had never been born.

So it is certainly "normal" for your child to tease and be teased. But it is also important to establish clear adult parameters around this painful process. It is normal for children to be jealous of their younger siblings, too, but we don't let toddlers drown their newborn brothers, however much they may fleetingly wish to. In much the same way, children need to be protected from acting out the full harshness of which they are capable toward each other.

## Preventing Problems with Other Children

While there is no way to keep your child from ever being hurt by his peers, there are some strategies that can help make these occurrences less likely and less frequent.

### Keep Open the Lines of Communication

In the interest of continuing communication, get to know your children's friends, at least by first name, and make the effort to become acquainted with their parents as well. It means finding or making some relaxed time on a daily basis during which your child can tell you about his day. For many parents and children, this time is in the car. While Mom or Dad is driving, and facing straight ahead, the child is less embarrassed by eye contact. That's when he or she seems to feel freer to ramble on about "Me and Roger, we was fighting and that's how I got this bump here" or "Then Sally told Megan that Claire is *Rachel's* best friend now, so of course Alison was just crushed"—or whatever the day's events may have been. Your role at this point is just to listen, make a few empathic comments ("That must have hurt"), and refrain from dismissing the child's problems. Some of the advice we too often give children—"If you are nice to someone, she will always be nice to you," "Everyone in your class is your friend really," and so on—has more to do with adult anxiety than with the reality of childhood. If you find yourself tempted to shut down the conversation in this way, remind yourself that it is OK for your child to have a bad day or to not get along with everyone. Life is not a greeting card, and it is not in your child's best interests to pretend it is. The important thing to establish is just that your child can and will talk to you—about the downs as well as the ups.

## Make Your Own Values Crystal Clear

Your child is listening to and learning from you, even when he doesn't seem to be. Make it clear that you do not think it is OK or amusing to tease another child about being fat. Make your own opinion of hitting or malicious gossip quite plain. The point is not to punish your child for whatever happened out on the playground—most of the time the story you hear will be so confused as to make it impossible to establish whose fault something was—but to educate. Watch your own language, too, for careless comments you might make about others. Your children are always listening, and they will model themselves on your attitudes.

## Celebrate Being an Adult, Freed from the Popularity Quest

Sometimes I see parents who are as concerned as their children are about being "popular." These are usually parents who still have intense feelings about their own childhood experiences. It will actually be more beneficial to your child if you can supply the sense of proportion that she can't supply for herself because she is still a child. Here are the kinds of adult comments that can supply proportion:

- "I used to worry about being excluded, too. Now that I'm grown up, I just walk away from people like that."
- "That word 'popular' is so strange. We used to talk about people being 'popular,' too. But most of the time I didn't like the supposedly 'popular' people nearly as much as I did my own real friends, and I don't suppose anyone else did, either!"
- "I got teased in school, too. It hurt at the time, but now I am proud of my red hair—you know it runs in our family."

Rather than relive your childhood struggles through your child, enjoy being a grown-up, and let your child see that adulthood is an island of comparative sanity she can look forward to reaching.

## Teach Some Simple Verbal-Defense Skills

Comments like "What did you say? My nose is ugly? Thanks for the compliment," "Oh, get a life," "Takes one to know one," and "Yeah, right, whatever you say" will not earn you, as an adult, a reputation for dazzling wit. Nevertheless, they are more effective than most remarks children can come up with on their own. When your child describes a teasing incident, role-play with him a little and make some suggestions about snappy comebacks. For a timid child, it can be a major victory just to have the ability to say, "I don't like it when you talk to me like that" and then walk away. And for an argumentative child, learning a few strategies for leaving the area before a physical fight breaks out can be equally useful.

## When More Is Needed
## for Dealing with Peers

All children get teased, but only some children get teased consistently. In some situations the time comes to intervene more forcefully:

• **If the roles don't rotate.** In our opening example, Maggie has been excluded by Jennifer and Caitlin. Jennifer has more or less annexed Caitlin, who was formerly Maggie's ally. If Maggie retaliates by forming an alliance with another little girl and excluding Jennifer and Caitlin, the game stays approximately even. It would not be unusual, for example, for Maggie and Jennifer to be best friends next week, excluding Caitlin. But if your child seems always to be the one excluded, then this is a bigger problem. If other parents and teachers complain that it is nearly always your child doing the excluding, that, too, is a problem.

• **If the language mirrors toxic adult categories of exclusion.** If your child is being teased with racial or religious epithets, with homophobic venom ("fag," "dyke," and other such epithets), or about an actual disability (burn scars or a limp, for example), intervention is needed. This would certainly also be true if you caught your child using such epithets or displaying such attitudes toward other children.

Your first round of intervention can sidestep the common dilemma: that is, where the parent wants to intervene but the child begs to handle the situation by herself. That is because your first, and often most effective interventions, need not look like interventions at all. These first steps include four kinds of intervention.

## Invite Other Children and Their Parents to Your Home

You need not provide a special occasion or fancy entertainment—just make a point of contacting the other children's parents, and inviting them and their children over to your house. The occasion can be for cookie baking, to watch a special television show, to play Monopoly; most any excuse will do. It is sufficient if the parents just drop the children off, as long as all the children get to see you chatting pleasantly with their parents at drop-off and pick-up times. Especially in the elementary years, proximity breeds friendship, and parents who get along will encourage children to get along. Having others in your home also gives you a natural chance to discuss differences— for example, that at your house you have a menorah instead of a Christmas tree, or you listen to classical music with your son instead of tossing the football around. And, finally, when you invite other children over, you have an informal chance to watch your child play with them, which is our second recommendation for an intervention.

## Observe Your Child with Other Children

If your child could describe to you why she gets excluded, she might be able to fix the situation. That she has no idea why the snubbing happens is part of the problem. By unobtrusively watching her at play, however, you may discover that she comes across as too bossy (which many oldest and only children do) or as overly friendly (children tend to avoid someone who appears very eager for friends; it's like a single who exudes desperation on a date). There may be a simple explanation that has been overlooked, such as your son simply speaks too softly to be heard while the other, more exuberant children are shouting. Being able to discreetly observe can help you solve the mystery.

## Talk with Other Parents and Your Child's Teachers

Other adults will have noticed the same patterns that you have observed. They may be able to provide you with valuable insight, as when the mother of one of my daughter Rachel's playmates confided to me that she always told her own daughter, "I wish your grades were more like Rachel's." Suddenly it was clear why the other little girl always stopped speaking to Rachel at report-card time. Even if the situation is not so easily resolved, when you have talked with other parents and with teachers, they will later be more willing to support you in putting together an educational program when one is needed.

## Educate Youngsters About Tolerance

When you are hearing racial, religious, or homophobic comments; vulgar sexual references; or insensitive comments about disabilities, it is appropriate for all the adults involved, parents and teachers alike, to plan an educational program to address these topics. Rather than naming any one child as the designated victim ("You all should quit talking to Christina like that; she can't help having a cleft palate"), plan the program to be more informational or general. It can include guest speakers and simple, clear education ("Christina's mother is here today to teach us about what a cleft palate is and how it gets fixed over time, along with Dr. Hawkins, who had a cleft palate himself as a child and is now a prominent craniofacial surgeon"). Children have a natural curiosity, which works in your favor here; anything that is talked about becomes less toxic.

## When Peer Relations Turn into an Emergency

If you have tried these suggestions but still are not getting support from the other adults, speak up to ask for help. It is appropriate for other parents to be concerned if their children are hurting your child; it is not appropriate if they mirror their children's narrow-minded attitudes. It is appropriate for teachers and school staff to actively intervene to educate kids and to promote positive social interactions. They should also be willing to intervene to prevent your child from being a scapegoat, even to the extent of moving your child into a new class, with a new set of children, if things do not improve.

We hope and expect that most of the time these suggested interventions will fully resolve the difficulties. But while it is rare, it has happened that parents find their child is truly in the middle of a hostile, dangerous environment. A recent Supreme Court case involved a little girl who for years endured physical groping and vulgar sexual taunts from a classmate, with the teacher and even the principal refusing to intervene.[1] The family was awarded significant damages, and it is to be hoped that there are no more situations out there like that. But we would be remiss not to cover your alternatives should such an extreme situation arise.

If your child is repeatedly hit or threatened physically; taunted with racial, religious, or sexual epithets; or sexually harassed, by all means protest loudly. Call the community department of your local police station and contact your child's school administrator. Police departments have community liaison officers these days for just this type of thing. And sometimes a phone call from a police officer convinces a parent that her child's taunting of others really is a problem, more quickly than will any number of phone calls from you or a teacher.

If the situation does not improve—that is, if you feel you are not getting support from school officials and other parents; if your child begins to experience sleeplessness, frequent nightmares, bedwetting or soiling (after being continent for some time), or if she has feelings of despair—by all means consider moving the child to another school. You can move to another public school by writing a letter explaining the situation to the district superintendent and stating your desired choice of new school. If you encounter any difficulties, an accompanying letter from a professional (such as your child's pediatrician), confirming your report of the child's distress, can expedite matters.

You have grounds for a lawsuit if your wishes are not heeded, and the district officials know this, which means they are likely to cooperate with you. If you want to move your child to a private school, religious schools are usually smaller and safer, though you should check out the school personally. In this type of situation, clergy can usually be appealed to for a scholarship or tuition reduction. Again, a letter from a supporting professional—a pediatrician or child and family therapist or psychologist—speaking to the child's distress, can be most useful in obtaining such aid.

If you don't want to or can't move your child from the school, you can also consider bringing in an advocacy organization from outside. The U.S. Department of Education is man-

## Problems with Teachers

**U**se this exercise to help you remember what it is like to have problems with your teacher. Imagine the worst day you have ever had at work. Now visualize that you are finally getting off work and coming back home. You can hardly wait to tell your spouse or significant other about your day. Consider how you would react if your spouse said to you:

- "If your boss was mad at you, I'm sure she had a good reason. I don't want to hear any more about it. And just for that, for getting in trouble at work, I am taking away your home computer and the CD player in your car."
- "Oh, you poor baby. Don't worry, I have already called and resigned you from your job, and I'll find you a nice new one on Monday. Of course, I don't know anything about your field, but I'm sure I can find some nice people for you to work with. Don't worry about a thing, just go lie down and take a nap."
- "Sounds like you had a bad day. I am always so impressed with how you handle these things; I learn a lot from how you deal with stress. Is there anything I can do to help?"

dated to protect the civil rights of schoolchildren, and I have known this federal agency to send out strong and effective professional advocates to back up parents whose children are not being treated fairly. Depending on the nature of the taunting, a specific advocacy organization (The Anti-Defamation League, NAACP, NOW) may be an appropriate advocate on behalf of your child.

If you catch your son or daughter being cruel to another, younger child or to an animal (being cruel to someone or something more helpless, as others have been cruel to him or her), do express your dismay. Also take that as a signal to move even faster to get your child out of the toxic situation or to bring in help from outside. If you end up moving your child, talk with the new school officials right away about the bad situation you came from, and be sure you have their full cooperation. The tone of peer interactions within a school can be greatly enhanced by a concerned principal who is willing to make this a focus.

If these responses represent three different spouses, to which one would you prefer to be married? A child's parents are his most significant others. What do you sound like to your child when he complains about his day?

## What's Normal in Relating to Teachers?

In elementary school, the teacher is an intense focus for most children. As a parent, you may even experience some mild feelings of jealousy, usually along about third grade, when it is common to hear children worshipfully remarking, "We have to recycle because Mrs. A. told us to," or "Miss B. likes chocolate; let's buy her some." Although male teachers are unfortunately rare in elementary schools, when present, they are likely to evoke even more intense loyalties: "Mama, I know you think that's the right answer, but that's not how Mr. G. explained it to us. And he knows."

This hero and heroine worship does not prevent elementary-age children from complaining that their teachers are too strict or favor other children, of course, and on a day-to-day basis the child may be cross with his teacher now and then. But overall you should expect a positive, warm relationship with the teacher in the elementary years. These are the teachers who teach your child about learning, who perhaps influence your child's future more than anyone else besides you. Most elementary school teachers have a real sense of vocation about their work, which is fortunate given how hard they work. They spend a great deal of uncompensated time in planning lessons and organizing their classrooms, a great deal of money out of their pockets on reward stickers, school supplies, and the like. And still they have to put up with such comments as "So what do you do? Just read stories all day?"

In middle school, it becomes "cool" for the child to have a more detached relationship with her teacher. The teachers most admired often meet this need by being more detached themselves, perhaps calling the children by their last names instead of their first names (and certainly never calling them "honey" or "sweetie," appreciated as that was back when that special third- or fourth-grade teacher used those endearments). Middle school children even delight in a certain amount of sarcasm, as long as they are not the targets of the day. They are not as tough as they would like us to think, however, and paradoxically these may be the years when they most need a sense that their teachers really do care about them. Middle school teachers who genuinely enjoy their students; who can sound hip and cool, yet simultaneously convey that they care; who can be patient with their students' emotional ups and downs; who can keep order, yet allow for age-appropriate socialization; who can accept that some days their charges will be too distracted by puberty to remember their own names, let alone the assigned reading—these teachers are worth their weight in gold and should be paid accordingly. They have the consolation of being fondly remembered in adult life. And they are rare, especially in some schools. It can happen, given how difficult it is to teach this age, that most educators teaching in a given middle school are even awaiting transfer to either an elementary or a high school.

High school teaching begins to more closely resemble college teaching in that the focus is more on the subject and less on the student. Still, the high school teacher who can set a rigorous academic standard, yet allow enough space and time to get to know his students personally, is often most appreciated. Children of this age still need guidance, and they can benefit greatly from a close relationship with a concerned teacher. At this age, the process begins to more nearly resemble adult mentoring.

## Preventing Problems with Teachers

As in helping your child deal with peer problems, it is important to keep open the lines of communication to help your daughter or son talk about teachers. Some special rules apply to conversations about teachers, though.

### Try to Not Take Sides

Parents tend to err in one direction or the other with this one. Some parents routinely double punish: that is, if a teacher reprimands the child and the parent learns of it, the parent will back up the teacher by administering a second punishment at home. This is done with good intentions, to reinforce the school's authority. But there is no quicker way to ensure that your child will stop talking to you about what happens at school. Also, given that you weren't there in person, you often have to rely on your child's version—and it is possible that your child might be right at least occasionally. Perhaps Mr. G. really did blame your child for something someone else did, or Mrs. A. may really have been in a bad mood. Teachers are human, too, and mistakes do occur. Reinforcing your child's sense that adults are being unjust by double punishing is not useful to him.

On the other hand, assuming that your child is always an angel will probably be even less useful to her. No matter how convincing the child's story is ("I wasn't doing one single thing, and suddenly he started yelling at me"), those of us who have worked with school-age children know that, without the child's actually lying, relevant information is sometimes mysteriously omitted. "Oh, well . . . yeah, I guess I was throwing the wastebasket at Johnny's head right about the time my teacher started yelling. I forgot about that part. But Johnny had it coming." Your best bet is to remember that you were not there, and you do not know exactly what happened. So you can be most useful by keeping the focus on what to do now, on problem solving.

## Express Empathy for Both Sides

You can probably really appreciate how mortified young Frank felt (in the example given at the opening of this chapter) when Mr. Green intercepted his note to Angela. If you were Frank's parent, it would help him greatly to hear that empathic feeling from you. At the same time, even if you don't agree with how Mr. Green handled the situation, as an adult you can appreciate that he has to keep order in the classroom in some way. Having all the boys and girls in class focusing on each other instead of his lecture is really not a viable option for him. Frank does not have the benefit of your adult perspective, however, and it would help him if you expressed deep sympathy, and then went on to also explain what it might be like to be Mr. Green, charged with maintaining order in a classroom full of active adolescents.

## Move On to Problem Solving

You have empathized with poor Frank. You have encouraged him to consider the possibility that Mr. Green had a viable point of view, also. (Frank probably wasn't able to hear much of that now, but he will store it away for future reference and perhaps then open himself up a little to another viewpoint.) Now, at a moderate to rapid speed before the conversation lags or degenerates into mere verbal abuse of the absent Mr. Green, ask Frank what he plans to do. Express your confidence in him, and encourage him to think about how he has solved similar situations in the past.

## Support Viable Alternatives and Express Confidence

Well, Frank's original thought was to leave town forever. But as you and he brainstorm about it, perhaps he can come up with some more viable alternatives. He may remember, with your help, the time he wrote a letter to the newspaper and how it was published. Perhaps he could compose an eloquent letter to Mr. Green explaining how much he resents the way the situation was handled. Perhaps he could make the letter so eloquent, he would *want* Mr. Green to read it out loud. (He could check the spelling first.)

Or maybe he wants to forget about Mr. Green, and just call Angela and commiserate with her. After all, she did say after-

## Family Activity

Spend a week making it a point to say something you appreciate about each member of your family every day, and encourage your children to let you know what they appreciate about you. We all need praise and hugs.

ward that she was sorry to have laughed and that Mr. Green was mean. Maybe, after all, this worked to get Angela's attention. (Some guidance about more appropriate ways to approach young ladies than discussing their degree of heat would be useful here, of course, especially if you are Frank's mother and can speak from the female perspective. Young teenage boys often get the wrong impression from music videos, watching impossibly lovely dancers swoon over a crudely talking male musician and imagining that the same sledgehammer approach will impress girls of their own age in real life. A little reality testing is in order: Those dancers get paid a lot of money to act impressed.)

Sooner or later, Frank will come up with an idea you can encourage. You should keep on expressing your confidence in his ability to overcome the problem. This takes patience on your part, but it teaches Frank useful skills for handling difficult bosses in later life. It's OK to get mad, he learns, OK to talk about your feelings, but then you try to see the other guy's point of view and move on to some ideas for solving the problem.

## Share Your "War" Stories

Probably you have had your own share of instructors, employers, or supervisors who were difficult for you, at least at times.

It can be useful for your child to hear you discuss that openly and honestly, especially if you keep the focus on how you surmounted the difficulty.

# When More Is Needed in Dealing with Teachers

Something you want to consider is how frequently these problem incidents repeat. If last week Mr. Green praised Frank for a good class presentation, and next week it is Frank's friend Bob who is the target of Mr. Green's humorous monologue, that is one case. But if Frank is the constant butt of Mr. Green's jokes, and Mr. Green has nothing good to say about him, that is another type of situation. In elementary school, it is a viable option to observe in the classroom. By middle and high school, your coming to watch is so embarrassing for your child as to defeat the purpose. But at any age, you can convene a meeting. If the interaction seems stuck, if your child is always angry with a particular teacher or the teacher with your child, ask that teacher to meet with you and your son or daughter.

## *Go to the Meeting as a Facilitator, Not a Judge*

It will not be helpful to you to set up the meeting to confront the teacher, without ever having heard the teacher's side. Nor is it likely to be useful to structure the meeting as a chance for you and the teacher to scold your child simultaneously. You can have maximal chance for success at the meeting by telling both your child and the teacher, in advance and again at the start of the meeting, that you are there only to help them work this out with each other. Ask questions about each person's viewpoint, express empathy for both sides, and encourage the two parties most directly involved (that is, the child and teacher) to come to a new understanding. If you think you will have difficulty doing this, ask the guidance counselor to come in and help you.

## Encourage Your Child to See the Teacher as a Real Person

With great difficulty, Frank may be able to consider that Mr. Green does have a legitimate interest in encouraging students not to pass notes. It probably has never occurred to Frank, however, that Mr. Green might have been having a stressful day or that Mr. Green was himself once a teenage boy. A teacher, too, needs to get to know his student as a whole person. Mr. Green knows Frank as a good student who sometimes goofs off. He may be completely unaware that he and Frank share an interest in fly-fishing or that Frank has no sisters and doesn't really know much about girls yet. You can't force a friendship, certainly, but it can be helpful to spend a little time at the meeting just getting to know your child's teacher. Even outside of the meeting, at back-to-school night and other such events, you can make a point of chatting with Mr. Green—and relaying to Frank additional evidence that Mr. Green is a real person, with a life outside the eighth-grade classroom.

## Role-Play Problem Solving

Especially after you have observed the interactions at the meeting, you may be able to help your child figure out more productive ways to talk with and to his teacher, new strategies to try. After all, you have been dealing with supervisors many more years than your child has. Try helping your child by role-playing these other ways of talking with a teacher.

# When a Problem with a Teacher Becomes an Emergency

When a teacher has a fixed, unchanging view of your son or daughter that is sharply at odds with your own, you have a serious problem. In no small part, this is because you have unwittingly set up a conflict of loyalty for your child. If the teacher thinks one way, and the parent another—and the disagreement is strong—the child cannot fully engage with school. Let's look at some steps to try in this eventuality.

### Bring in a Third Party to Mediate

This time, don't invite your child to the meeting. Let it be a polite, but honest, discussion between you and the teacher about your differences of opinion. And ask the guidance counselor to mediate. If this meeting is not successful or you feel the guidance counselor is equally closed to your position, it is perfectly acceptable to bring in another third party of your own choosing (such as a family therapist who has discussed the situation with you, a trusted clergyman, or your child's Little League coach—someone who knows him in another context). Do make sure whoever you bring in understands professional confidentiality and can be trusted with this private information about your child's struggles.

### If It Still Doesn't Work, Fight or Switch

If repeated meetings have failed to make significant headway in resolving the differences, you have a decision to make. You can consider changing your child to another school. Or you can bring in an outside advocate. This should be the first step, instead of the last, if a teacher has hit your child, made sexual advances to your child, used a racial or religious epithet, or repeatedly called your child "stupid" or other demeaning names. This is unprofessional behavior, no matter what your child was doing. The outside advocate can be an attorney, but as discussed under "Problems with Peers," he or she can also be a representative of the Department of Education or of an advocacy organization.

## Problems at Home

Check out from the library a stack of foreign-language tapes or a book on learning a language you don't know. Try studying the new language at home, in a peaceful setting, when you are relaxed. Now try studying while standing on the curb near a busy highway during rush hour. How much could you concentrate, do you think, if you were actually out on the highway, dodging moving vehicles? Most of us cannot concentrate well on learning when we do not feel safe. For a child, her family is her safety. How well do you think your child can concentrate if the family seems about to crash and burn?

## What's Normal in Relationships at Home?

In today's world, most children will have to deal with change and crisis. Only 42 percent of children in the United States live in a two-parent family; divorce and remarriage have become the norm in many schools. It is not our intent to encourage you to beat yourself up emotionally because your family life is not always perfect. But it would be unfair to your child not to consider how her stability is being affected. Just as you could not learn a foreign language while dodging traffic on a busy street, so also your child cannot learn without a stable, safe context at home. Children have to be rooted in stability before they can grow out into the outside world.

## Preventing Problems at Home

While problems at home inevitably affect a child's school life, there are some strategies to help cushion the impact.

### Let Your Child's Teacher(s) Know What Is Going On

Aunt Hilda died. You and your husband are separated. You and your wife have been divorced for many years, but you are just now starting to date again. These are the kind of intimate events most of us don't share with outsiders. But while your child is in school, the school is not an outsider. If you don't inform teachers at least of the major events in your child's life, they may not understand a change in his behavior. What looks like carelessness (lost books, homework not completed, untidy appearance) would be handled differently if the teacher knew, for example, that a child's mother was in the hospital.

Teachers and school officials are professionals, sworn to confidentiality. You should be able to feel safe trusting them with this kind of family information. In middle and high school, if you feel uncomfortable with the number of teachers you would need to notify or don't know all your child's teachers well, it is acceptable to notify your child's guidance counselor about family stresses. In elementary school, it works best to let the homeroom teacher know directly. If you are uncomfortable talking in person, or don't want to encourage a lot of questions, a brief, factual note will do fine.

## Let Your Child Know What Is Going On

My favorite story about how important it is to let children know about family problems concerns the young daughter of a highly conflictual couple. Both mother and father were afraid to tell their eight-year-old daughter that they were divorcing, despite the facts that they had lived apart for nearly a year and the process was well under way. They were also convinced that she knew nothing about the impending divorce. When I was skeptical about the idea that she really knew nothing, they asked me to meet alone with their daughter, to assess her awareness of the events in her parents' lives. I began by asking the little girl if she had any questions for me. "Yes," she replied politely, "I was wondering if you could explain the difference between a community-property state and an alimony state. I think it may affect my mother's settlement." Evidently she had been listening in on phone calls to attorneys.

The moral of this story is worth repeating—and even capitalizing: YOU CANNOT SUCCESSFULLY KEEP SECRETS FROM YOUR CHILDREN. True, children need to hear information in age-appropriate ways, and there is no need to give them extra information they don't want or need. It is sufficient, for example, to know that Mama is sick and the doctors are trying to help her get better; the four-year-old doesn't need to know the statistics on the type of cancer involved. It is enough to know that Mom and Dad are getting a divorce because Mom thinks Dad spends too much time away from home, and Dad does not agree with that idea; it is not necessary or desirable to speculate with an eight-year-old about what

Dad is doing when he's out late at night with his female friends. You can—and should—share with your twelve-year-old your sad feelings about the death of your own mother, and how your personal religious beliefs are sustaining you through this difficult time; it is not essential to get out the encyclopedia and compare beliefs across all the world's religions, especially if you are not feeling up to it.

It really *does not work* to try to evade altogether even the most difficult issue. In the absence of a convincing, true explanation, young children tend to blame themselves ("I must have made Daddy go away by being bad") and older children tend to simplistically blame one person (as Emily blames Dan in the example at the opening of this chapter). False or evasive explanations from adults around them just exacerbate this tendency in youths. You create more problems than you solve when you tell your child that Grandmother just went for a long trip (Why did she do that? Where? How could a loving grandmother just disappear like that? Who's going to disappear next?) or that Mama just needs to lie down for a rest (Why does Mama need to lie down all the time now? Is it because the four-year-old did something bad and tired her mother out? If this is the child's understanding, then what kind of guilt will that four-year-old have if Mama dies?).

Worst of all, what happens when you say that Mom and Dad still love each other just the same, nothing is wrong, there is no disagreement, but they are just not "in love" anymore and so will be living apart. This last explanation, while it still gets recommended to divorcing parents trying to be civilized, is quite possibly the most frightening thing you could tell a young child. The distinction between "love" and "in love" is meaningless to a child. What the child hears is that people stop loving each other for no apparent reason, and therefore have to live apart. No child can hear that without instantly fearing that this will happen between her and her parents—that they will stop loving her, since this can happen for no reason, and throw her out on the street. I remember the great difficulty a young father had in explaining to his preschool children that their mother had left him, and them, to go live with a motorcycle gang. But when he haltingly got out that Mama had decided to live with her new friends all the time now, and that he didn't like her new friends and so wouldn't go along with that, his little boy burst out, with infinite relief, "Oh, is that all! We already knew about that. We know you don't like Mama's friends with beards and she does. But we thought *love* goes away, not just Mama goes away with her friends."

Love doesn't go away. Sometimes adults can't agree, and therefore, painfully, have to agree to disagree. When an adult and a child disagree about something, the relationship is not at risk; if the adult feels strongly enough, he or she can set a limit. But adults can't always set limits on each other, so it could happen that adults have to agree to disagree and live apart. Painful as that reality is, it is a lot better than a sugarcoated lie that leaves the child confused and terrified. The specifics of the irreconcilable disagreement can be sketched in for the child in age-appropriate detail. (If there is no irreconcilable difference, then perhaps Mom and Dad need to try harder to work things out.)

## When More Is Needed at Home

Don't let problems and differences rise to the level of an emergency. Qualified help is available. When family problems threaten to become overwhelming, consult a family therapist. Qualified practitioners in your area can be recommended by the American Association for Marriage and Family Therapy.[2] Long-term therapy may not be needed; often, a few sessions are sufficient to get things back on track. You know you need to consult with a professional when you notice one or more of the following:

- You feel overwhelmed.
- You feel very sad.
- You are having a lot of trouble sleeping.
- You and your child no longer enjoy each other or have fun together.
- You start to feel hopeless or bitter over arguments in the family.
- You have the same arguments over and over.
- Every time one situation improves (Johnny starts doing better in school), another situation in the family gets worse (now Suzie is having trouble).
- You just can't figure out what is going on that's causing all the problems.

Connections between therapist and client are a personal matter, and you don't have to stick with the first therapist you try if you don't "click" with that person. Keep trying until you find someone whom you feel is really listening.

Get some help; you'll be glad you did.


## A Word of Warning

Whether youngsters are unhappy over friends, teachers, or family, they are impulsive by nature. Young teens in particular can be desperately unhappy one minute, and cheerful again the next. It is difficult to predict their moods. For this reason we urge everyone reading this book who has children living at home to remove all firearms from the home. A moment's murderous rage or a half hour of acute misery will pass, leaving the child just that much further along on the road to maturity. But that same fleeting emotion can have disastrous consequences if, during that brief time, the child has access to a loaded gun and with it can hurt himself or someone else. Then the consequences can never be undone. Even if you are absolutely sure your child will never have a moment's instability, even in the volatile early teenage years, you cannot possibly answer for all your child's friends who might have access to your home. We implore you to keep guns and ammunition far away from children.

---

### TEACHER TIPS

These tips may help you and your child to work with teachers to compensate for or overcome unhappiness at home and school.

#### Keep the Teacher Informed

As your child's teacher, I may not know that your child is having problems with me or with his peers if you don't tell me. And I almost certainly won't know about problems at home. Give me a chance to help; don't assume there is nothing I can do.

#### Encourage Letter Writing

I like to encourage kids to write me a letter and place it on my desk. Then there is no interruption, and I can get to him privately to respond. A kid did that last week to tell me that the other boys in class don't seem to like him. I asked how

I could help, and he didn't really know. So I just spoke generally to the whole class about how hurtful it is to exclude others, and we talked about times they had felt excluded. But later I may choose a boy to befriend him, or find some way to single him out in class in a positive way, to help him look good to the others. Letters are a good way to communicate privately about sensitive matters. (And I would never read a child's letter out loud in class, even if I intercepted one to another child.)

### Look to Resources Outside School

Church and temple youth groups, after-school activities, volunteer mentors like the Big Brother/Big Sister program—these are all worthwhile resources to explore beyond the school and home.

### Consider What Movies and TV Contribute to Children's Feelings

I taught a boy in Idaho who became afraid to go to school after watching a horror movie. He was afraid that when he came home from school, his family would all be dead—because that was a scene from the movie. That's an extreme situation, but just as you would censor having weapons in the home, screen out movies and TV shows that vividly depict bloodshed, suicide, homicide, tragedy, and madness. You should especially screen these when your child is going through difficult enough times already. Violent video games are something else to watch for questionable content—there are some unbelievably trashy ones on the market, with spurting blood, women getting raped, and other horrors. Look for the ratings on the package, and go for the ones marked "E" (a designation meaning that it is acceptable for everybody). Read the box as well to be sure the content is acceptable to you. Sometimes, in fact, it's good just to forget all that: just turn off the TV, radio, and computer, and sit down to have a nice hot cup of cocoa together. Life is hard enough without a constant stream of negative stimulation coming at you.

**Get Help When You Need It**
We all need help at times. There is no shame in asking for it.

# Resources

## *For Problems with Peers*

See www.teasingvictims.com, a website run by a young man who was himself teased for years; he figured out how to make the teasing stop, and now he shares his tips with other children in a warm, enjoyable way. See also easingtheteasing.com, a guide for parents who want to help their children get over various problems with peers. A good book is Douglas Bloch, *Positive Self-Talk for Children: Teaching Self-Esteem Through Affirmations* (New York: Bantam Books, 1993).

## *For Problems with Teachers*

Guy Strickland has written a funny and practical guide for parents struggling to know when to intervene and when to stay out of a teacher-child relationship. This book will be useful for older children to read on their own as well.

Guy Strickland, *Bad Teachers: The Essential Guide for Concerned Parents* (New York: Pocket Books, 1998).

## For the Family

Bill Doherty has written a lovely and thoughtful book that may give you good ideas on how to improve your family together time. See William Doherty, *The Intentional Family: How to Build Family Ties in Our Modern World* (New York: Addison Wesley, 1997). There are also on-line support groups, which may be just what you're looking for: For families with children grieving the death of a loved one, see www.funeral.net/info/chilgrf.html. For parents struggling with divorce issues, go to www.divorce.net. For single parents, see www.parentswithoutpartners.org. For military families, especially those facing a separation, a good site to visit is www.sgtmoms.com. And for Canadian parents, see www.canadianparents.com. There's a special website for mothers who also work outside the home: www.moms~refuge.com. Finally, some general on-line parenting communities include these three: www.parentsoup.com, www.parentsplace.com, www.parents.com.

# Epilogue
## In Search of a Village

When my mother was ten years old, she and her best friend, Patty Jo, decided to start smoking. With practiced bravado they asked at the corner store for cigarettes, explaining the purchase was "for our mothers." Now, Mr. Grady, proprietor of Grady's General Store, knew perfectly well those cigarettes were not for any adults. My mother's mother never smoked, and Patty Jo lived with her grandmother; Mr. Grady was familiar with the exact circumstances of both children. As my mother told me, back in Marion, Kentucky, in the 1930s "Everyone knew everything about everybody." So Mr. Grady was acting with calculation when he sold the girls his strongest, least-filtered cigarettes. It is reasonable to conclude that he knew these would make my mother and Patty Jo violently ill, as indeed they did. His parting comment, "Now you all be careful with these," therefore takes on the nature of a warning. Had the experiment not resulted in a lifelong aversion to smoking—which it did—he would have refused to sell them any more cigarettes. Mr. Grady never even considered calling up my mother's mother or Patty Jo's grandmother; in that time and place, every adult assumed a casual responsibility for every child. The incident remained between Mr. Grady and the girls, who had to clean up the alley behind the store after they got done being sick there.

Back then, Marion functioned as a village, "a group of contiguous dwellings, bound by a common and simple organization." Part of that common and simple organization was an unspoken, implicit set of rules that created a safety net for the children of the community.

By the 1950s, when my brother at age four chased the babysitter with a stick, some things had changed. The neighbors in that Texas suburb did not expect to become involved. Even the elderly and somewhat inept babysitter, indignant at such treatment, felt that it was not her role to administer the punishment she considered my brother so richly deserved. Instead, she called my mother to come home from her dinner party. My mother, not my father, came home—by then it was already clear that children were the primary parent's responsibility, not the community's as a whole, not even the family's as a whole.

But my mother had a community of other mothers to fall back on. Specifically, she had the Sewing Club. The "contiguous dwellings" were no longer a factor, but the "common and simple organization" still was. It was supplied by the majority of mothers, staying at home and raising their children most of the time, who were available to and for each other. My mother's six best friends met weekly to darn, mend, and plot strategy. When this child-raising crisis arose, the Sewing Club naturally took it under consideration, just as they had dealt with Val's son's school problems or Ann's daughter's shyness. In consultation with them, my mother devised the plan of assuring my brother she would never, ever leave him again until he was ready to behave responsibly with other adults. After a week or so of her relentlessly undivided attention and constant company, even at nursery school, he was only too ready to promise good behavior with future babysitters.

Thirty-five years later, I sat by my telephone longing for the Sewing Club. At the time, my daughter Rachel was seven. I had just had her placed in a special enrichment class for "gifted" children one hour a day, my initial victory after her terrible kindergarten year. She and her best friend, Alexander, who also went to enrichment class, were walking down the hall to lunch one day. They were discussing what they had just learned about electricity. They had learned that wood does not conduct it, and metal does. They were curious about plastic. Simultaneously, they spied a plastic fork on the floor near the lunchroom. It was near an uncovered wall outlet. The same idea apparently occurred to both. Alexander demonstrated his superior intellect and his rightful placement in enrichment class by suggesting that since Rachel, my daughter, had smaller fingers, she should be the one to plunge the fork into the outlet. She did so.

Fortunately, she was not electrocuted. However, when she subsequently artlessly informed her teacher what she had done, the possibility that she might have been hurt occurred to everyone. So did the unpleasant necessity of calling an electrician to fish out the by-now melted plastic fork from inside the outlet.

The school called me at home, where I never am at midafternoon on a weekday. Then they called me at work, but the secretary they reached knew only that I was teaching, not where. Naturally this only added to my sense of guilt later on.

When I went to pick up my child at her aftercare program that day, she seemed unusually subdued. "Mommy," she confessed, "I did something very bad. I almost burned the school down." Only half attending as I was, and knowing her to be typically a conscientious child, I began reassuringly, "Now, honey, it probably wasn't all that bad. . . ." Midway through that sentence, the dread words "burned the school down" hit my tired brain.

That first hour of shifting from my faculty job to my parent job was a challenging hour at the best of times. On this particular day, it clearly called for a glass of wine while I interrogated. I did not get the full story all at once, but I gathered enough to understand that this was serious. The several phone messages from school officials on my answering machine helped me get that point.

Sooner than usual, Rachel went to bed, her guilt relieved by confession and by her implicit faith that I would surely know what to do next. I, however, stayed up, looking at the telephone and wishing there was someone to call for advice. Was she too old to spank? Was she too young to understand the consequences? Would I cripple her burgeoning scientific curiosity if I punished her too harshly? On the other hand, would she end up doing time in Leavenworth for arson if I was too lenient? I wanted the Sewing Club to take up my case. I would even have been glad to see Mr. Grady.

I wanted to call my mother, but she has her own very different life now: she was in Australia with her new husband. I had not yet remarried. I did call Rachel's father, my ex-husband, to apprise him of the situation. He felt I must be speaking of some child other than the angel he sees on weekends: "She never does this kind of thing when she's with me." My married friends tell me their current spouses have been known to manifest the same incredulity. Nor, in fairness, could he be expected to know what to do any more than I did.

My friends today are work friends who are readily available for a discussion of university policy, but they happen to be childless or to have children of very different ages than Rachel.

The rest of my family is scattered and far away. My neighbors don't know me, or I them. My child's school is excellent, brisk, and urban—fair to all, but partial to and personally involved with no child. In short, I live in a city, not a village, and there is no common, simple organization to which I can turn.

I was up most of the night longing for a village. Early the next morning, I got a phone call from my child's enrichment-class teacher, Mrs. Goldman. She was calling, she told me, unofficially. "Officially, Rachel will have to meet with the assistant principal and see about a consequence," she explained. "But unofficially, I just wanted to see if you think she understands. I love that child like she was my own daughter, and I told her over and over, 'Rachel, I don't care if you do burn the school down, I just don't want you to kill yourself!' She has to be more careful! Do you think she understands?" As I listened to her warm, not official, not impartial, human voice, tears came to my eyes. "Will you be my village?" I asked her.

Fortunately, I don't think she heard me. It would have been difficult to explain. But in the absence of a common, simple organization (provided for us along with our contiguous dwellings), that uncommon but purposeful connection between people who mutually care for and about a child becomes more important. It becomes worth finding and creating such connections. Indeed, it becomes essential to do so.

With Mrs. Goldman's help, a punishment was worked out to fit this particular crime. (For the remainder of the school year, Rachel had to be escorted through the hall by two third graders, thus ensuring her safety. This was a humiliation, she has assured me, unprecedented in human history, and it has so far prevented any further experiments while on the school premises.) But I do not imagine that this was the last time I will feel the need of community as I raise my children. And I am very glad to have enrichment teachers, specially trained teachers who care and understand about children like my daughter, with whom I can discuss her.

The great secret about advocating for your child is that you are advocating for yourself as well. You are creating for yourself a community of others, people who see your child the way you do, who become your allies in the common task of educating your child. What you are actually doing is reclaiming Mr. Grady and the Sewing Club, in our time, in ways that now fit our lives. So keep up the good work. And be sure to keep us posted! E-mail us about your struggles and your triumphs at our website, www.schoolsolutionstalk.com.

# Endnotes

## Introduction

1. Jacobs, J. C. "Effectiveness of Teacher and Parent Identification of Gifted Children as a Function of School Level." *Psychology in the Schools* 8 (1973): 141. See also subsequent articles on this issue, available on-line through www.hoagiesgifted.org.
2. The U.S. Department of Health and Human Services. *Report of the Secretary's Task Force on Youth Suicide.* Washington, D.C.: U.S. Department of Health and Human Services, 1989.
3. Lynd, Robert, and Helen M. Lynd. *Middletown.* New York: Harvest Books, 1929.
4. The U.S. Bureau of Labor Statistics, available on-line at http://stats.bls.gov/blshome.htm.
5. *Coalition for Marriage, Family, and Couples Education (CMFCE), Smart Marriages Research Archive*, statistics available on-line through the research archive at www.smartmarriages.com.
6. The United States Bureau of Labor Statistics, available on-line at http://stats.bls.gov/blshome.htm.
7. To view the act in its entirety, see www.ed.gov/offices/OSERS/IDEA.

# Chapter 1

1. Orozco, Cynthia. *Rodriguez v. SAISD*. The Handbook of Texas On-line, 1999. This is available at www.tsha.utexas.edu/hand book/online.
2. See http://ncacs.org.
3. See www.tutor.com.
4. See www.home-school.com (Homeschool World), and www .home-ed-press.com (The Home School Resource Page).

# Chapter 2

1. West, J., K. Denton, and E. Germino-Hauskin. *America's Kindergarteners: Findings from the Early Childhood Longitudinal Study, Kindergarten Class of 1998–1999, Entry Fall 1998*. Washington, D.C.: U.S. Department of Education, 2000.
2. See www.ed.gov and click to the topic "homework."
3. Log on to the home page of the American Association for Marital and Family Therapy, www.aamft.org, and click on its therapist-locator service to find qualified family therapists near you who are specialized in the areas you request.

# Chapter 3

1. National Association for the Education of Young Children (NAEYC). *Young Children*, NAEYC Position Statement on School Readiness, November 1990, 21–23.
2. The Irlen Institute may be reached at 562-496-2550.
3. Nurss, Joann. *Readiness for Kindergarten*. Urbana, Illinois: ERIC Clearinghouse on Elementary and Early Childhood Education (ED291514), 1987. For an on-line assessment of developmental readiness and related resources, see www.kidsinc.com.

4. For an interesting discussion of this issue, see JoEllen Perry's article "What, Mrs. Crabapple Again?" in the May 24, 1999, issue of *U.S. News and World Report.* This is available on-line at www.usnews.com/usnews/issue/990524/nycu/retain.htm.

5. The Gesell Institute of Human Development is located at 310 Prospect Street in New Haven, Connecticut. Its series of books by Ames and Ilg, *Your Five Year Old, Your Six Year Old,* and so on, is highly regarded by professionals in the field. Any book in the series may be ordered by calling 203-777-3481 or using the on-line site at Barnes and Noble (www.bn.com).

6. See www.ldpride.net. Click on "learning styles," then on "multiple intelligences." See also Gardner, H. *Multiple Intelligences: The Theory in Practice.* New York: Basic Books, 1993.

7. See http://surfaquarium.com/im.htm.

8. Look in the telephone book for those places *not* accredited as colleges, and then check with the Better Business Bureau about their reputation.

# Chapter 4

1. See www.hoagiesgifted.org.

2. See www.starchefs.com. This site also contains a longer interview with Reed Hearon.

3. There is debate on this subject—see both www.hoagiesgifted.org and britesparks.com for further discussion of this issue.

4. See www.gtworld.org and click on "links."

5. Click on "resources" at www.hoagiesgifted.org for a long list of summer, Saturday, and distance programs. See also "links" at www.gtworld.org.

6. Pen pal matches for gifted children can be found at www .eskimo.com/~user/zpenpal.html. Several other types of pen pal programs are also offered.

## Chapter 5

1. United States Department of Education, Office of Educational Research and Improvement, National Center for Education Statistics. *The National Assessment of Educational Progress 1998 Reading Report Card for the Nation and the States.* Washington, D.C.: Department of Education.

2. This statistic is taken from a summary of the reading research of Drs. Joseph Torgeson and Richard Wagner at Florida State University. This research was funded by the National Institute of Child Development. The full text of the report is available online at www.research.fsu.edu/ResearchR/fallwinter9899/features /phonics.html.

3. This statistic is taken from the testimony of Dr. Reid Lyon, the acting chief of the Child Development and Behavior branch of the National Institute of Child Health and Human Development, a component of the National Institutes of Health. Dr. Lyon was testifying before Congress about the NICHD-funded research into reading problems among United States schoolchildren. The full text of his testimony and recommendations to Congress is available at www.ldonline.org/ld_indepth/reading/nih_report .html.

4. Weaver, C. *Eric Digest #93: Phonics in Whole Language Classrooms.* Washington, D.C.: ERIC Clearinghouse on Reading, English, and Communication, Department of Education, 1994.

5. See www.research.fsu.edu/ResearchR/fallwinter9899/features/ phonics.html.

6. Ibid.

7. Lehman, N. "The Reading Wars." *Atlantic Monthly,* November 1997.

8. Testimony given to Congress by Dr. Reid Lyon.

9. See www.research.fsu.edu/ResearchR/fallwinter9899/features/ phonics.html.

10. See www.research.fsu.edu/ResearchR/fallwinter9899/features/ phonicshook.html.

11. At www.members.aol.com/dyslextest, you can test your child and, for a fee that is less than private psychological testing (about $140), you can have a report of the results delivered to your child's school. Similar options are available at www .scientificlearning.com.

12. Raskind, M., and E. Higgins. "Assistive Technology for Post-secondary Students with Learning Disabilities: An Overview." *Journal of Learning Disabilities* 31 (1998): 27–40.

13. Ibid.

14. Good places to start are Family Village (www.familyvillage .wisc.edu), The Council on Exceptional Children, special education division (www.cec.sped.org), and The National Center for Learning Disabilities (www.ncld.org).

15. See www.pave-eye.com.

16. See www.ldpride.net.

17. See www.ldpride.net and click on the learning-styles exam.

18. For sample mind maps, more about how they are used, and to order books and products related to this idea, go to www .mind-mapping.com.

# Chapter 6

1. This is a statistic from Lawrence Diller, author of *Running on Ritalin* (New York: Bantam Books, 1998). For updates see www.docdiller.com.

2. LeFever, G., K. Dawson, and A. Morrow. "The Extent of Drug Therapy for Attention Deficit Hyperactivity Disorder Among Children in the Public Schools." *American Journal of Public Health* 89: 9 (1999): 1350–1364.

3. The American Psychiatric Association. *The Diagnostic and Statistical Manual of Mental Disorders*, fourth edition. Washington, D.C.: American Psychiatric Association, 1994.

4. Diller, Lawrence. *Running on Ritalin*. New York: Bantam Books, 1998.

5. Ibid.

6. See www.chadd.org.

7. Arnold, L. Eugene. "Treatment Alternatives for Attention Deficit Hyperactivity Disorder." As presented at the National Institutes of Health Consensus Development Conference on Diagnosis and Treatment of Attention Deficit Hyperactivity Disorder, National Institutes of Health, Bethesda, Maryland, November 16–18, 1998.

8. National Institutes of Health. "Diagnosis and Treatment of Attention Deficit Hyperactivity Disorder." *National Institutes of Health Consensus Statement* 16: 2 (November 16–18, 1998): 1–37.

9. Diller, Lawrence. *Running on Ritalin*. New York: Bantam Books, 1998.

10. See a discussion of this at www.abcnews.go.com/sections /living/DailyNews/ritalin980416.html. See also the counterbalancing viewpoint at www.nimh.nih.gov/publicat/adhd.cfm# adhd10.

11. See Peter Breggin's website, www.breggin.com.

12. See www.borntoexplore.org for a discussion of this viewpoint.

13. Carroll, L., and J. Tober. *The Indigo Children: The New Kids Have Arrived*. Carlsbad, CA: Hay House, 1999.

14. See www.breggin.com; for an opposing viewpoint, visit www.chadd.org.

15. See www.breggin.com.

16. See www.nimh.nih.gov/publicat/childqa.cfm for questions and answers on this topic.

17. Jensen et al. "The Multimodal Treatment Study of Children with ADHD." *Archives of General Psychiatry* 56: 12 (1999).
18. Arnold, L. Eugene.
19. Ibid.
20. Phelan, Thomas. *1-2-3 Magic: Effective Discipline from 2 to 12*. New York: Child Development Press, 1996.
21. See www.childu.com and www.independent-learning.com for complete on-line curriculums, kindergarten through eighth grade, and kindergarten through twelfth grade, respectively. These are commercial operations with tuition comparable to private schooling.
22. To find a qualified biofeedback practitioner, ask your family doctor, dentist, or your state's medical society. Biofeedback practitioners should be medical professionals with special training in the modality.
23. To get a more complete description of the modality or to locate a practitioner in your community, contact www.interactive metronome.com

# Chapter 7

1. *Davis v. Monroe County School Board*—see Findlaw Internet Legal Resources website for the full text of the court's decision.
2. Log on to www.aamft.org and click on the therapist-locator service. Or look in your local Yellow Pages under marriage and family therapist and note those therapists with AAMFT-approved credentials.

# Additional Readings

The references listed in the endnotes and resource guide for each chapter will help you further explore the issues raised in that chapter. The additional readings listed below are less specific to any one type of school problem but interesting and informative for all concerned parents.

## Exploring the Educational System

Cutler, W. *Parents and Schools: The 150 Year Struggle for Control in American Education*. Chicago: University of Chicago Press, 2000.

Ravitch, D. *Left Back: A Century of Failed School Reforms*. New York: Simon & Schuster, 2000.

*Both these books will provide thought-provoking historical background on the forces that have shaped your child's school.*

Murphy, J., and B. Duncan. *Brief Intervention for School Problems: Collaborating for Practical Solutions*. New York: Guilford Press, 1997.

*While this book is written for counselors and teachers, the positive examples and generally optimistic tone may give you some encouraging ideas as well.*

At www.mhkids.com, parents can sign up for a free bimonthly newsletter that reports on educational trends and news for parents.

*This informative newsletter may help you recover from any pessimism induced by the first two, more historical books. This website also offers a wide range of educational resources parents can use at home to support or augment what is being taught at school, including phonics and enrichment materials.*

## Exploring Ways Parents Can Help

Cullinan, B. *Read to Me: Raising Kids Who Love to Read.* New York: Scholastic, 1992.

*This is a practical guide to encouraging reading, including locating optimal books for every age and interest.*

Gianetti, C., and M. Sagarese. *Cliques: 8 Steps to Help Your Child Survive the Social Jungle.* New York: Broadway Books, 2001.

*Of particular interest to parents of middle schoolers, but valuable at all ages, this book gives suggestions for how parents can intervene tactfully but firmly in their children's social lives.*

Gold, L., and J. Zielinski. *Homeschool Your Child for Free: More than 1200 Smart, Effective, and Practical Resources for Home Education on the Internet and Beyond.* Roseville, CA: Prima Publishing, 2000.

*Despite the title, this exhaustive compendium of resources will be useful for parents who don't home-school as well.*

Saavedra, B. *Creating Balance in Your Child's Life.* Lincolnwood, IL: Contemporary Books, 1999.

*The author provides a guide to assessing your child's individual temperament and suggests outside activities that will enrich, not exhaust, your type of child and your family as a whole.*

# Exploring Your Child's Future

Problems in school need not mean problems in adult life. Here are options to investigate with your older child.

At www.myjobsearch.com, click on "career planning." Over fifty detailed assessments (tests and surveys) are offered, to help older teens and young adults pinpoint their career interests and skills. Almost all are free of charge and can be taken and scored on-line. A few are geared to middle schoolers as well.

Also at www.myjobsearch.com, the career planning bookstore offers most of the forty titles available in the acclaimed VGM Careers for You series. This series of books outlines careers of interest to particular "types," for example the romantic, the class clown, the kid at heart, the outdoor type, and so on. Each book explains how something that may now be perceived as a weakness (such as being shy or talking too much in class) may be an indication of a possible vocational strength and goes on to describe the education and experience needed for each type of job within this area of strength. These practical and enjoyable guides are also available on www.monster.com, in bookstores, and through the publisher (VGM Career Books).

Pope, L. *Colleges That Change Lives: 40 Schools You Should Know About Even if You're Not a Straight A Student.* New York: Penguin, 2000.

*This guide to off-the-beaten-path colleges includes a useful section on colleges for the learning disabled and special colleges designed around special interests.*

# Index